# *Disturbing*
# THE UNIVERSE

# *Disturbing* the Universe

POWER AND REPRESSION IN

ADOLESCENT LITERATURE

by Roberta Seelinger Trites

UNIVERSITY OF IOWA PRESS ψ Iowa City

University of Iowa Press, Iowa City 52242

Copyright © 2000 by the University of Iowa Press

Printed in the United States of America

Design by Richard Hendel

http://www.uiowa.edu/~uipress

Portions of chapter 4 first appeared as "Queer Discourse
and the Young Adult Novel: Repression and Power in Gay
Male Adolescent Literature," *Children's Literature Quarterly*
23 (1998): 143–151. Reprinted with permission of the
Children's Literature Association.

Portions of chapter 5 first appeared as "Narrative
Resolution: Photography in Adolescent Literature,"
*Children's Literature,* 27. New Haven: Yale UP, 1999. 129–
149. Reprinted with permission of Yale University Press.

The publication of this book was generously supported by
the University of Iowa Foundation.

Printed on acid-free paper

Library of Congress Cataloging-in-Publication Data
Trites, Roberta Seelinger, 1962–
Disturbing the universe: power and repression in
adolescent literature / by Roberta Seelinger Trites.
p.    cm.
Includes bibliographical references and index.
ISBN 0-87745-732-8 (cloth)
1. Young adult fiction, American—History and
criticism.    2. Adolescence in literature.
3. Postmodernism (Literature)—United States.    4. Power
(Social sciences) in literature.    5. Repression (Psychology)
in literature.    6. Teenagers—Books and reading.    I. Title.

PS374.A3T75    2000
813.009'9283—dc21

                                00-037422

00  01  02  03  04  C  5  4  3  2  1

*For George Major, with love*

# Contents

# Preface

I remember complaining to a friend in 1975 that I was tired of reading the books in our middle school library because "they're all about kids with problems." Maybe with that succinct analysis of the 1970s problem novel, I damned myself to a lifetime of studying adolescent literature. In any event, trying to understand the genre as a whole was certainly part of my motivation for taking a college course on the subject in 1980. The teacher, Dorothy Van Riper, commented at the time on the inadequacy of critical materials in the field. Another professor, Lilian R. Furst, mentioned the same problem in a graduate seminar I had in 1984 (a seminar in which I was regarded as the resident field expert, having only recovered from adolescence the week before the course started). By the time I was safely past adolescence in 1992, a senior colleague of mine—Taimi Ranta—raised the same concern about the dearth of criticism in the field. Since I have been thinking about these issues so long, it seems fair to say that this book has been twenty-five years in the making.

I did not reach any real breakthrough in understanding the genre, however, until I began teaching the course myself in 1994. From my own studies, I had expected to find many rites of passage and initiations, patterns of growth, conflicts, Oedipal crises, confessional first-person narrators, and identity crises. But as I taught the course, I began noticing other recurring patterns in these books, some of which seemed predictable and others that did not. Books for adolescents are subversive—but sometimes only superficially so. In fact, they are often quite didactic; the denouements of many Young Adult novels contain a direct message about what the narrator has learned. Moreover, books for adolescents have lots of sex. And many dreadful parents. Many photographers. Many schools. Many dead bodies. (In a course that included *Adventures of Huckleberry Finn, The Outsiders, The Chocolate War, Toning the Sweep,* and *The Pigman,* one class counted more than fifteen deaths in the first five weeks of the semester.) Books for adolescents have many ideologies. And they spend much time manipulating the adolescent reader.

Eventually, I realized that these lists of predictable and unpredictable patterns in adolescent literature share one thing. They can all be linked to issues of power. Although the primary purpose of the adolescent novel may appear to be a depiction of growth, growth in this genre is inevitably represented as being linked to what the adolescent has learned about power. Without experiencing gradations between power and powerlessness, the adolescent cannot grow. Thus, power is even more fundamental to adolescent literature than growth. During adolescence, adolescents must learn their place in the power structure. They must learn to negotiate the many institutions that shape them: school, government, religion, identity politics, family, and so on. They must learn to balance their power with their parents' power and with the power of the other authority figures in their lives. And they must learn what portion of power they wield because of and despite such biological imperatives as sex and death. Foucault tells us it is in the very nature of power to be both enabling and repressive because it is omnipresent: "power is everywhere; not because it embraces everything but because it comes from everywhere" (*History* 93). His words can be modified to fit books about adolescence: in adolescent literature, power is everywhere.

Yet somehow, the critical study of adolescent literature has developed as a field without any great reliance on some of the poststructural theories that best help explicate the issues of power in the books that teenagers read. Caroline Hunt offers one explanation why this has happened. She suspects that because many of the critics who teach college courses on adolescent literature are often training teachers, professors tend to focus on topics that are commonly accepted as pertinent to pre-service teachers, such as issues of censorship or identifying the literary elements of a novel (11). But if we engage the poststructural theories that help us to understand the transactions between text, reader, and culture, we can become more astute readers, teachers, and critics.

Theories that invite us to be sensitive to language and how it constructs the individual, theories that raise our awareness about race and class and gender and adolescence itself as social constructs, theories that demonstrate the relationship between narrative structures and ideologies, and theories that help us to position the reader can work together to help us discern how the elements of adolescent literature establish intricate patterns that reinforce the contradictory positions of adolescents within our culture.

Indeed, adolescents occupy an uncomfortable liminal space in America. Adolescents are both powerful (in the youthful looks and physical prowess that are glorified by Hollywood and Madison Avenue; in the increased economic power of middle-class American teenagers as consumers; in the typical scenario of teenagers succeeding in their rebellions against authority figures) and disempowered (in the increased objectification of the teenage body that leads many adolescents to perpetrate acts of violence against the Self or Other; in the decreased economic usefulness of the teenager as a producer of goods in postindustrial America; in the typical scenario of teenagers rebelling against authority figures to escape oppression). It is no wonder that the body of literature linked to this population pursues the exploration of power relentlessly.

The opening chapter of this study, then, includes a study of some of the pivotal issues that have historically informed adolescent literature, the first of which is the nature of power. I next investigate definitions of "adolescent literature," including a focus on the Young Adult novel (that is, the novel specifically marketed to an adolescent audience) as a subset of the broader genre about adolescents, adolescent literature. Finally, I trace the historical study of the *Bildungsroman* as a way to contextualize the development of the YA novel as a postmodern phenomenon. My goal in this chapter is to provide the reader with a sense of the literary patterns and the history of ideas that have led to the existence of Young Adult literature.

In the second chapter, I explore only four of the many institutions that demonstrate how central power is to the adolescent experience in novels: politics, school, religion, and identity politics (including race, class, and gender). In books—as in life—institutions both empower and repress adolescents in the ways that they create new opportunities for teenagers while they simultaneously establish rules within which the teenager must operate. For example, government politics and the politics of identity are forces that shape adolescents in YA novels. As teenagers learn more about themselves politically, they can often understand themselves better—and paradoxically, they express themselves less freely. Schools and organized religion are also institutions that work actively to mold the adolescent into appropriate degrees of power within a culture. Virtually every YA novel depicts the adolescent in conflict with at least one of these types of institutions. Innumerable institutions that regulate power exist in adolescent literature, but because they are infinite in number, I leave it to the reader to further identify them.

Chapter 3 traces how power struggles that exist between individuals and institutions give rise to multiple conflicts between adolescents and authority, another arena of the literature with infinite possibilities. Two types of authority are especially pertinent to YA novels: authority within the text and the authority of the author over the reader. Within the text, authority is often depicted as a struggle with a parent or a parent substitute, so I rely on psychoanalytic theory to trace the inevitability of this particular conflict in adolescent literature. This conflict with authority that is embedded in most texts for adolescents in turn provides the author with opportunities for using ideology to manipulate the adolescent reader. In that sense, authors themselves become authority figures in adolescent literature. The mechanisms by which they manipulate the reader to assume subject positions that are carefully constructed to perpetuate the status quo bear investigation. And because of this, YA novels themselves serve as yet another institution created for the purpose of simultaneously empowering and repressing adolescents.

Chapters 4 and 5 explore how sex and death, as biological imperatives, both empower and repress in adolescent literature. Such social constructions as heterosexuality, homosexuality, and lesbianism give rise to depictions of sexuality that explore its ideological and discursive nature. Similarly, death has a great discursive presence in adolescent literature. Death serves as a particularly intricate example of how power is deployed in YA novels because it has a thematic function and a narrative function for the adolescent reader; that is, the adolescent's increased understanding of life as limited by death is a predominant theme in the literature, but this theme also affects the narrative line of many novels for teenagers. Thus, death affects the form as well as the function of many novels marketed to teenagers.

My conclusion is an appeal for the inclusion of poststructural methodologies in classrooms that employ adolescent literature. Because YA literature has been so influenced by postmodernism, the genre lends itself well to poststructural methodologies, although many teachers have been thus far reluctant to employ these reading strategies in the classroom. Relying on what has worked in my own teaching, I provide an overview of how scholars of adolescent literature have successfully employed reader response theory, historicism, multiculturalism, feminism, Bakhtinian readings, psychoanalytic theory, Marxism, and narrative theory. Far from being a complete survey of the field, this chapter is intended to demonstrate how these theories can be used in the classroom rather than serving as an exhaustive review of the literature.

The novels I have included in this study are also very much influenced by those I have taught in my own classroom. I rely on several books that I think work well to demonstrate the patterns in adolescent literature: *Adventures of Huckleberry Finn*, *Little Women*, *The Catcher in the Rye*, *A Separate Peace*, *The Outsiders*, *A Wizard of Earthsea*, *The Chocolate War*, *Is That You, Miss Blue?*, *Breaktime*, *Lyddie*, *Toning the Sweep*, and *Weetzie Bat*. James Bennett, Francesca Lia Block, Judy Blume, Bruce Brooks, Aidan Chambers, Robert Cormier, Chris Crutcher, Peter Dickinson, Lois Duncan, Nancy Garden, Virginia Hamilton, S. E. Hinton, M. E. Kerr, Norma Klein, Ursula K. Le Guin, Madeleine L'Engle, Margaret Mahy, Robin McKinley, Walter Dean Myers, Richard Peck, Daniel Pinkwater, William Sleator, Beatrice Sparks, Mildred Taylor, Cynthia Voigt, Barbara Wersba, Jacqueline Woodson, Laurence Yep, and Paul Zindel are among the many authors writing in English who have created texts that are in one way or another pivotal in the Anglo-American YA canon. Some of these authors are either unrepresented or underrepresented in this text because of space considerations. Nevertheless, all of them depict adolescents disturbing and being disturbed by the institutions that construct their universe.

I am blessed in the number of people who have supported the writing of this book. Certainly it would not exist were it not for the initial encouragement of two of them: Pamela Riney-Kehrberg, who urged me to write the sabbatical proposal that became the foundation of *Disturbing the Universe*, and Holly Carver of the University of Iowa Press, whose confidence in me made both *Waking Sleeping Beauty* and this book possible. Equally supportive were the staff of the College of Arts and Sciences at Illinois State University. They listened to me, protected my time, and did so much of my work while I was writing that it feels as if this book were the result of the entire team headed by Dean Paul Schollaert and including Richard Dammers, Peggy Haycraft, Sandi Krumtinger, and Judy Marshall. I thank them all with unstinted gratitude.

Numerous scholars have provided me with invaluable feedback, but I am especially grateful to the readers of the earliest drafts of the manuscript who were all most generous in sharing their comments with me: Mike Cadden, Karen Coats, Sherri Inness, Jill May, and Anita Tarr. Nancy Tolson, Anne Phillips, Bonnie Shaker, Peter Hunt, Betty Greenway, Joel Chaston, Linda Benson, Phyllis Bixler, Mark West, Caroline Hunt, Michelle Martin, Vanessa Wayne Lee, Kara Keeling, Maria Nikolajeva, Elizabeth Keyser, Lois Kuznets, Kenneth Kidd, Rebecca Saunders, David Rudd, Marilynn Olson, Gillian Adams, Claudia Nelson, Jean Stringam, Naomi Wood, Betsy Ford, Ginny Carroll, Laura Davis-Clapper, Phil Nel, Bob Broad, Teresa Higus, Steve Meckstroth, Denise Anton Wright, Pam Day, and Christie Lau all provided pivotal feedback at key stages of the manuscript's development. Ron Fortune, Betty Chapman, Rodger Tarr, Jan Neuleib, and Al Feltner have also been consistently supportive.

Because *Disturbing the Universe* originated from my teaching of English 375, Adolescent Literature, at Illinois State University, I would be remiss not to mention at least a fraction of the students who influenced my thinking about adolescent literature over the years, including Jenny Abraham, Tim Ballard, Deborah Brothers,

Molly Burdette, Ronn Byrd, Julie Fraser, Heidi Green, Joellen Handling, Sundown Handt, Cortez Harris, Amy Hutchinson, Candy Jendro, Caroline Jones, Melissa Juvinall, Karla Kelly, Greg Maier, Lori Marable, Mike Martin, Ryan McCrae, Amanda McMenamin, Aamon Miller, Kathy Moore, Wanda Myers, Michelle Ochs, Val Perry, Kim Plattner, Lesley Powers, Temecka Russell, Dana Scott, Julie Semlak, LeKeya Sherrill, Leslie Shobe, Shawn Staley, Becky Thomason, Laurie Walczak, Owen Williams, and Dan Zehr. I regret that I cannot name all of the more than two hundred students who deserve to be listed here.

The friends who served as midwives to this project were Susan Burt, Lisa Choate, Cindy Christiansen, Elizabeth Davis, Margaret Haefner, Laura Pedrick, Pam Riney-Kehrberg, and Pat Witzig. They supplied me with the caffeine, the e-mails, the good reading, the advice, and the laughter I needed to get through the labor of writing a book and balancing the rest of my life. Just as important were the sanity-saving friends who allowed me to sing with them: Sally Parry, Bob McLaughlin, Rick Martin, Tak Cheung, Tony Otsuka, Mary Williams, John Hatle, and all the members of the Music Club.

But my deepest thanks go to the person who never complains about my writing *or* my singing: my husband, George Seelinger. Without him, most of what I value in this life would not be possible.

# *Disturbing*
## THE UNIVERSE

### CHAPTER I

# "Do I dare disturb the universe?"

## ADOLESCENT LITERATURE IN
## THE POSTMODERN ERA

And indeed there will be time
To wonder, "Do I dare?" and, "Do I dare?"
Time to turn back and descend the stair,
With a bald spot in the middle of my hair —
(They will say: "How his hair is growing thin!")
My morning coat, my collar mounting firmly to the chin,
My necktie rich and modest, but asserted by a simple pin —
(They will say: "But how his arms and legs are thin!")
Do I dare
Disturb the universe?
   (excerpt from "The Love Song of
   J. Alfred Prufrock," by T. S. Eliot)

T. S. Eliot was in his early twenties and undoubtedly still feeling the diverse effects of adolescence when he published "The Love Song of J. Alfred Prufrock," his poem about a Hamlet-like middle-aged man who is immobilized by indecision. At its core, the poem asks a question as germane to adolescents as it is to the middle-aged: "Do I dare disturb the universe?" Given that many teenagers wonder if they should or even can affect the world in which they live, Eliot has captured the essence of adolescence when he has his narrator pose the question.[1] In the context of adolescence, Prufrock's question reflects the desire that many teenagers have to test the degree of power they hold. Because at its heart this question "Do I dare disturb the universe?" is about power, it serves as an apt metaphor for what adolescents often seek to know about themselves.

Jerry Renault takes up this question in Robert Cormier's *The Chocolate War* (1974). Jerry hangs in his school locker a poster of a man walking alone on a beach that bears the caption "Do I dare disturb the universe?": "Jerry wasn't sure of the poster's meaning. But it had moved him mysteriously" (97). *The Chocolate War*

explores the question of whether Jerry can disturb the universe
—of what will happen to him if he dares to assert his personal
power. Jerry is a student at Trinity High School, a Catholic boys'
school that is involved in a fund-raising candy sale. The acting
principal, Brother Leon, invites the school's unrecognized but
powerful vigilante fraternity, The Vigils, to participate in the sale,
which they agree to do in an effort to increase their power over
other students. The Vigils have a tradition of meting out "assignments" to haze students: Jerry Renault's first assignment is to
resist Brother Leon's efforts to make him sell the chocolates
for ten days. Jerry accepts the assignment but then disturbs the
universe of Trinity High School when he continues refusing to
sell the chocolates past the ten days of his assignment, even after The Vigils have ordered him to begin selling the candies
again. He is the first student ever to resist The Vigils. In a final
showdown, Archie, the leader of The Vigils, and his sidekick
Obie manipulate a boxing match in which Jerry is ritualistically
slaughtered.

Jerry's final words in the novel echo the novel's opening statement, "They murdered him." His final lines are unspoken thoughts
that he directs to his friend Goober: "Do whatever they wanted
you to do. . . . They tell you to do your own thing but they don't
mean it. They don't want you to do your thing, not unless it happens to be their thing, too. . . . Don't disturb the universe, Goober,
no matter what the posters say. . . . Otherwise, they murder you"
(187). Although Jerry appears defeated and is even possibly dead
by novel's end, the book still answers the question affirmatively:
yes, he can disturb the universe. In fact, he *should* disturb the universe. Doing so may be painful, but Jerry has affected other
people with the choices he has made.

This intertextual question that lies at the heart of *The Chocolate
War*— "Do I dare disturb the universe?" — is representative of
an ethos that informs many adolescent novels. The chief charac-
teristic that distinguishes adolescent literature from children's literature is the issue of how social power is deployed during the
course of the narrative. In books that younger children read, such
as *Peter Rabbit*, *Where the Wild Things Are*, *Alice in Wonderland*, *Winnie-
the-Pooh*, *Charlotte's Web*, *Zeely*, or *Sarah, Plain and Tall*, much of the
action focuses on one child who learns to feel more secure in the

confines of her or his immediate environment, usually represented by family and home.[2] Children's literature often affirms the child's sense of Self and her or his personal power.

But in the adolescent novel, protagonists must learn about the social forces that have made them what they are. They learn to negotiate the levels of power that exist in the myriad social institutions within which they must function, including family; school; the church; government; social constructions of sexuality, gender, race, class; and cultural mores surrounding death. One critic of adolescent literature, Perry Nodelman, dismissively describes characters in adolescent fiction as people who "live ordinary lives, but see them in terms of melodrama" ("Robert Cormier" 102). Nodelman is undoubtedly reacting to the profound seriousness that many of these characters express in their first confusion about social institutions. In *The Chocolate War*, for example, Jerry Renault must negotiate his place within a family, in terms of a religion, and in his school. Jerry's epiphany is a recognition that social institutions are bigger and more powerful than individuals. The lesson he learns is a primary one in Young Adult literature.

Young Adult novels are about power. But they have not developed this tendency from within a vacuum. Thus, in this chapter I will explore four topics: power as it is defined in ways germane to adolescence; definitions of adolescent literature and the YA novel in the context of their historical evolutions; an investigation into the genres that have influenced the development of the YA novel, notably the novel of development and the coming-of-age novel; and the influence of such literary movements as romanticism and postmodernism on the depiction of adolescence in Young Adult novels. It is my contention that we can better understand the dynamic relationship in literature between characters and the institutions that define them if we also understand the history of ideas that affected the unique development of the Young Adult novel.

## Power

Before I go any further, I want to explore the concept of "power," both as I am using it and as others have used it, in ways that are pertinent to the study of adolescent literature. Max Weber defines power as "the possibility of imposing one's will upon the behavior of other persons [which] can emerge in the most diverse forms" (323). Weber focuses on economic power as the institutional power that dominates most people (323–324). Althusser broadens the definition of economic power, demonstrating how as Ideological State Apparatuses, institutions have a self-perpetuating interest in instilling their ideologies into the masses in order to retain their hegemony (155–157). Michel Foucault defines power as "that which represses" (*Power* 90), and he identifies power as ubiquitous: "Power is everywhere; not because it embraces everything, but because it comes from everywhere" (*History* 93).[3] Foucault contrasts two political definitions of institutional power. One he calls the "contract-oppression schema" (*Power* 92). It is based on the belief that all individuals hold a certain amount of power that they voluntarily relinquish to exist under the rule of a governing body (88). The other he calls the "domination-repression" model, in which the individual exists in "a perpetual relationship of force" (92). The latter of these views, and the one Foucault considers a more plausible explanation of social dynamics, defines power as a political force that is a function of the economy — of the forces of production — and so is in perpetual motion. Individuals do not possess power so much as they apply it in the process of trading market goods (98), so power "only exists in action" (89). Power is more a process than a commodity, according to him.[4] As a result, market forces repress the individual's power rather than individuals' power being oppressed by a sovereign.

If we believed the contract-oppression definition of power that Foucault rejects, we might say that in *The Chocolate War* Jerry Renault has power in agreeing to exist in harmony with the forces of oppression at Trinity High School, The Vigils and the teachers. He is defeated by novel's end because he has chosen to break the contract and so must be oppressed by the power structure. Foucault would say instead that rather than possessing a certain amount of power to begin with, Jerry actually exists in a chain of power, a chain that involves the selling of education as a commodity and that results in the commodification of the chocolates. Their sale is a means of production for the students. Jerry's power in the situation is fluid: he both has and does not have power, depending on his relationship to the market forces at specific points in the novel's time. When he overwhelms the market by providing a model for the other boys' nonparticipation in the means of production, the market retaliates by attempting to obliterate him in a "war." Foucault even supplies the term "war-repression schema" as a synonym for the "domination-repression" model of power; he makes much of the notion that "power is war, a war continued by other means" (*Power* 90). I think Foucault would enjoy Cormier's bellicose choice for a title, *The Chocolate War*.

Problems exist, however, with both Foucault's model of power and the one he rejects, in that neither allows for the individual's potentially positive power. Whether we think of people as oppressed by the state or by dynamic economic forces, we are focusing on power as something that conspires against them. An alternate way of thinking of power is in terms of subjectivity, in terms of the individual's occupation of the linguistic subject position. In *The Psychic Life of Power* Judith Butler promulgates such a definition of power in acknowledging that the individual "is at once formed and subordinated" (6) by power because "power not only *acts on* a subject but, in a transitive sense, *enacts* the subject into being" (13). As such, power is the force that allows for subjectivity and consequently, agency.[5] Moreover, power exists both externally and as the very source that constitutes the subject (15). Butler thus concurs with Foucault's analysis that power is a process, but her definition allows for an internally motivated subject who can act proactively rather than solely in terms of taking action to prevent oppression or repression. Butler might focus on the decision Jerry Renault makes when he utters the word "no," refusing to sell the chocolates (Cormier, *Chocolate War* 89). His action is a linguistic utterance and a conscious choice, and the textual commentary on his action is telling: "Cities fell. Earth opened. Planets tilted. Stars plummeted. And the awful silence" (89). Language here is a marker of power, especially because Jerry's loss of language represents a dramatic shift in the power structure at his school.

Lacan supplies another pertinent definition of power. Focusing like Butler on the interior formation of the subject and like Foucault on the exterior forces that repress the subject, Lacan describes individual power in terms of *assomption*: the individual's active assumption of responsibility for the role into which society casts her or him (Fink 46–48). As Lacan puts it, "one is always responsible for one's position as subject" ("Science and Truth" 7; quoted in Fink 47). Such a definition of power acknowledges both the external and internal forces that compete to empower and repress individual power, but it also allows for the individual's acknowledgment of one's power as a necessary function of subjectivity. When adolescents grapple with such questions as, "Do I dare disturb the universe?" they must reckon with both their sense of individual power and their recognition of the social forces that require them to modify their behaviors.

Lacan's thinking about power influences Karen Coats when she interprets *The Chocolate War*. She does so in terms of *assumption*, pointing out that Jerry Renault is an example of a person who assumes the position of Other into which he has been forced.[6] He starts out forced into a position that is painful, but then finds the pleasure in the situation by willfully accepting the enforced position. He has taken responsibility for the pain but also for the pleasure that he gets from the pain in being subjugated. Even as he is being annihilated by those who oppose him, he is victorious because he has done what he set out to do. He has assumed responsibility for the role of rebel into which the society of Trinity High School has cast him.

Feminist theorists such as Marilyn French also talk about power in terms of being enabled. French prefers a model in which people have "power to" do good rather than having "power over" other people to dominate them. She writes, "There is power-to, which refers to ability, capacity, and connotes a kind of freedom, and there is power-over, which refers to domination" (505). To a certain extent, I am interested in how adolescents are empowered (and disempowered) in terms that French uses: when are teenagers in Young Adult literature allowed to assume responsibility for their own actions and when do dominating adults refuse to acknowledge their capabilities? But the larger question for me is an investigation of the fluid ways that the individual negotiates with her or his society, with the ways adolescents' power is simultaneously acknowledged and denied, engaged and disengaged. As John Knowles writes in *A Separate Peace* (1959), "When you are sixteen, adults are slightly impressed and almost intimidated by you" (31). What, then, do adolescents do with that intimidating power?

The various definitions of power I have described work together to form a definition of power in adolescent literature. Adolescent characters exist in a "perpetual relationship of force" (Foucault, *Power* 92) created by the institutions that constitute the social fabric constructing them. Because they are defined within perpetual forces of power, power "enacts [them] into being" (Butler, *Psychic* 13). That is, the social power that constructs them bestows upon them a power from which they generate their own sense of subjectivity. As acting subjects, they assume responsibility for their position in society (Lacan, "Science and Truth" 7), whether they engage their power to enable themselves or to repress others (French 505). Power is a force that operates within the subject and upon the subject in adolescent literature; teenagers are repressed as well as liberated by their own power and by the power of the social forces that surround them in these books. Much of the genre is thus dedicated to depicting how potentially out-of-control adolescents can learn to exist within institutional structures.

## Defining and Historicizing the Genre

In trying to define adolescent literature, Sheila Schwartz notes that the American Library Association classifies adolescent literature into three categories: "Books Written Specifically for Adolescents," "Books Written for General Trade Market Which Have Adolescent Heroes and Heroines," and "General Books of Interest to Young Adults" (3). Elsewhere, I have referred to the first of these three categories as Young Adult novels, whereas I consider the three lists combined to constitute the whole of adolescent literature ("Theories" 2–3). Maria Nikolajeva observes that in many European countries, Young Adult novels are referred to as "jeans prose" because of their emphasis on such artifacts of material culture as "clothes, food, music, language" (62). YA novels are certainly a marketplace phenomenon of the twentieth century.[7] Adults create these books as a cultural site in which adolescents can be depicted engaging with the fluid, market-driven forces that characterize the power relationships that define adolescence. After all, publishers rather than teenagers bestow the designation

"YA" on these books. Even when authors have not intentionally
written for adolescents, they invariably portray adolescents engaged in a domination-repression model, so authors, too, are
complicitous in the process. Cormier, for example, maintains that
he did not write *The Chocolate War* for an adolescent audience
(Cormier quoted in DeLuca and Natov 110–111). But a trend has
emerged in the way YA novels rely on adolescent protagonists who
strive to understand their own power by struggling with the various institutions in their lives. This trend seems to be one of the
defining factors of the YA novel.

One reason that YA novels originated in the twentieth century
involves the history of adolescence. The word "adolescent" was
only beginning to come into common usage in postbellum America when such writers as Mark Twain and Louisa May Alcott were
writing (Kett 127), even if that is the age group they would have
wanted to identify as the primary audience for their most famous
novels. Products of the romantic movement's interest in youth,
Twain, Alcott, and scores of other authors available to American
readers (including Charles Dickens, Charlotte Yonge, James Feni-
more Cooper, Robert Louis Stevenson, Martha Finley, Susan War-
ner, Horatio Alger, and Susan Coolidge) wrote novels about youth
that appealed to teenaged readers. Youth readers in the first half
of the twentieth century found books by L. M. Montgomery, the
Stratemeyer Syndicate, Cornelia Meigs, Rudyard Kipling, Kate
Douglas Wiggin, Zane Grey, Frank Merriwell, and Mabel Robinson. But adolescence as a social concept did not gain the widespread attention of the American public until G. Stanley Hall's
*Adolescence* (1905) inspired four actions that Joseph Kett identifies.
Following Hall's advice, adults sponsored organized social activities (for example, Scouting) for middle-class teenagers, and
the concept of adolescence influenced school administrators to
grapple with the large numbers of teenagers who were entering
high school because industrialization had decreased their economic value on farms. Well-meaning theorists wrote a variety of
self-help books for parents seeking to understand their teenagers,
and they guided the vocational guidance movement that was designed to help teenagers negotiate the movement from school to
work (Kett 221). Adolescence as such did not become institutionalized in America until the twentieth century, so it stands to

reason that books marketed specifically to this demographic arose as a product of the twentieth century. The American Library Association and the National Council of Teachers of English also increased attention to the need for better reading material for school-age children, thereby influencing the caliber of books marketed to adolescents. Moreover, teenagers' increased economic resources and social autonomy in the robust economic years following World War II further increased their market power, making book publishing for older youths an even more attractive industry than it had ever before been.

Literature specifically written for and marketed to adolescents came into its own in America when World War II changed the country's economy nearly forty years after Hall's work called attention to adolescence as a psychological phenomenon. Literary historians frequently cite one of three dates as turning points for YA literature: 1942, when *Seventeenth Summer* appeared; 1951, when *The Catcher in the Rye* was published; and 1967, when *The Outsiders* was published.[8] Whichever of these texts a critic prefers to cite as the wellspring of YA literature, the fact remains that the genre defined itself in English-speaking countries in the two decades following World War II and was understood to be a distinct literary genre by the end of the 1960s.[9] Brown and Stephens note that the earliest manifestations of the YA novel may have evolved from the social unrest of the 1960s. They suggest that the lack of positive adult role models in such books as *The Outsiders* may well be what first defined the genre, but that as the genre has evolved, the depiction of adults and characterization in general, issues of diversity, the use of point of view, and thematic development have all become more complex (14–17). Nevertheless, few literary genres have had as compact an evolution.[10]

Young Adult literature shares many characteristics with books marketed to adults about adolescents. The major intersections between these two sets involve various types of novels about the maturation process, including the *Entwicklungsroman*, which is a broad category of novels in which an adolescent character grows, and the *Bildungsroman*, which is a related type of novel in which the adolescent matures to adulthood. *Entwicklungsromane* can be thought of as novels of growth or development, whereas *Bildungsromane* are coming-of-age novels that are sometimes referred to as "apprenticeship novels." [11] Understanding the history of literature about adolescence can help us to understand not only how Young Adult literature came to exist but also what its ideological and aesthetic functions are.

## *The* Bildungsroman *and the* Entwicklungsroman

Because YA novels evolved historically from the *Bildungsroman*, we need to understand the distinction between that term and the term *Entwicklungsroman*. The distinction proves useful in helping to position the YA novel within postmodernism, particularly because scholars of children's and adolescent literature have tended to overemploy the term *Bildungsroman* in recent years. For example, in *Children's Literature and Critical Theory*, Jill P. May questions whether the picture book *The Snowy Day* has a "bildungsroman pattern" because it has a "home–away–home" pattern (41). Although May decides the picture book is not a *Bildungsroman*, throughout her text she implies that all children's books about growth are *Bildungsroman*. But thought of that way, the definition of the *Bildungsroman* ceases to have meaning, because what children's book *isn't* about growth? Peter Rabbit grows. Max, King of the Wild Things, grows. Ramona grows. M. C. Higgins grows. Anne of Green Gables grows. Cassie Logan grows. Harriet the Spy grows. Christopher Robin grows. Granted, Nancy Drew and her compatriots in series fiction — paraliterature, as Maria Nikolajeva calls the genre (58) — do not necessarily grow. And some novels like Avi's *Nothing but the Truth* (1991) and Cormier's *The Chocolate War* problematize the issue of growth by leaving the reader wondering who, if anyone, has grown. But the idea of growth — the investigation of which characters have developed and which have not — is one of the most common principles in the study of children's and adolescent literature. Since novels of development are *Entwicklungsromane*, virtually all children's and adolescent novels participate in the genre. For purposes of clarification, I tend to refer to *Bildungsromane* as novels in which the protagonist comes of age as an adult. If I refer to a novel as an *Entwicklungsroman*, that is because the protagonist has not reached adulthood by the end of the narrative.

G. B. Tennyson traces the coinage of the term *Bildungsroman* to a German scholar named Wilhelm Dilthey (in 1870 in a biography of Friedrich Schleiermacher) (135).[12] Hans Heinrich Borcherdt built on Dilthey's definition when he formally defined the *Bildungsroman*: "first, there is a cultural goal, which is the complete unfolding of all natural qualities; then there is a clear path toward that goal. . . . in sum, the movement in the *Bildungsroman* is a reasonably direct line from error to truth, from confusion to clarity, from uncertainty to certainty, from, as the Germans have it, nature to spirit" (Tennyson 137). Goethe's *Wilhelm Meister's Apprenticeship* (1795–1796) is widely regarded as the first *Bildungsroman*. The concept of the *Bildungsroman* emerged in an atmosphere nurtured by the romantic belief in the individual. Only with the establishment of a widespread cultural interest in individuals' growth was the concept of adolescence defined psychologically or explored literarily. Jerome Buckley offers a standard and fairly intricate definition of the *Bildungsroman* in *Season of Youth*. He writes that in the typical *Bildungsroman*, a sensitive child grows up in a rural setting feeling confined by his entire family, but especially by his father, who cannot understand the boy's imaginative life. School also proves restrictive for the protagonist, so he leaves home to go to an urban center, where he is likely to have at least two romantic experiences, one of which has the potential to corrupt him and the other of which has the potential to purify him. His initiation is complete when, after much soul-searching, he triumphs over the trials he faces with his parents, with financial resources, with women, and accepts his own capacity for work and for love (18–23). Buckley, then, essentially defines a formula for novels about adolescence intended for adult readers.

In the original German construction of the term, the *Bildungsroman* is distinct from other genres in that it "presuppose[s] a more or less conscious attempt on the part of the hero to integrate his powers, to cultivate himself by his experience" (Howe 6). In other words, the protagonist's growth is neither accidental — as say, Peter Rabbit's is — nor simply a matter of normal developmental growth, as Moon Shadow's is in Laurence Yep's *Dragonwings* (1975); rather, the hero self-consciously sets out on a quest to achieve independence. The *Bildungsroman* is therefore an inherently Romantic genre, with its optimistic ending that affirms the protagonist's entry into adulthood.[13] Buckley identifies *David Cop-perfield*, *Sons and Lovers*, and *A Portrait of the Artist as a Young Man* as examples of Anglophone *Bildungsromane*.

One glaring problem with Buckley's definition (and Dilthey's and Borcherdt's and Tennyson's) is how androcentric it is. There is no place in these critics' definitions for a female protagonist, even though Buckley tries to fit Maggie Tulliver from *A Mill in the Floss* into the pattern. This proves to be something of a procrus-tean fit for someone trying to demonstrate that the *Bildungsroman* is about finding the capacity to love and to work (Buckley 22–23), since Maggie commits suicide at the end of Eliot's novel. Annis Pratt defines why male *Bildungsromane* patterns do not apply to women:

> In the women's novel of development (exclusive of the science fiction genre) . . . the hero does not *choose* a life to one side of society after conscious deliberation on the subject; rather, she is radically alienated by gender-role norms *from the very outset*. Thus, although the authors attempt to accommodate their he-roes' *Bildung*, or development, to the general pattern of the genre, the disjunctions that we have noted inevitably make the woman's initiation less a self-determined progression *towards* maturity than a regression *from* full participation in adult life. (36)

Because of a lifetime of living as Other, females experience "a division of loyalties between" their sense of authentic selfhood "and the social world of enclosure" (25). Pratt implies that there is basically no such thing as a female *Bildungsroman* when she says, "It seems more appropriate to use the term *Entwicklungsroman*, the novel of mere growth, mere physical passage from one age to the other without psychological development, to describe most" nov-els of female development; "it seems clear that the authors con-ceive of growing up female as a choice between auxiliary or sec-ondary personhood, sacrificial victimization, madness, and death" (Pratt 36). Elizabeth Abel, Marianne Hirsch, and Elizabeth Lang-land cite "inner concentration" (8) and intimacy with others (11) as the chief goals of female novels of development, which they divide into two patterns: the novel of apprenticeship, such as Mil-dred Taylor's Logan family chronicles or Voigt's Tillerman saga, and the novel of awakening, which is by definition a novel of an adult's rather than an adolescent's awakening. Catherine Marshall's *Christy* (1967) is certainly not a YA novel, but it is often read by adolescents, so it serves as one example. Abel, Hirsch, and Langland eschew the use of the term *Bildungsroman*, identifying it — as Annis Pratt does — as a suspect construct.

I support their assertion that we should take more care in using the term *Bildungsroman*, not merely in an effort to uphold some sort of precious academic hairsplitting, but because in distinguishing coming of age novels (*Bildungsromane*) from novels of development (*Entwicklungsromane*), we can pay more attention to the relationship between power and growth that shapes adolescent literature. Adolescents in *Bildungsromane* such as Katherine Paterson's *Lyddie* (1991) mature into adulthood. *Lyddie*, in fact, seems to follow Buckley's description of the *Bildungsroman* almost formulaically: sensitive Lyddie is emotionally orphaned by a father who has abandoned her and by a mentally ill mother who eventually dies. Although Lyddie is embarrassed about being functionally illiterate, she decides to journey from the family farm in Vermont and eventually arrives in the mill town Lowell, Massachusetts, where she is educated in a straightforward literacy narrative by her coworkers Betsy and Diana.[14] She has two sexualized encounters with men: the first is quite debasing when her foreman, Mr. Marsden, sexually harasses her; the other is closer to Buckley's definition of the purifying romance in that Lyddie's neighbor Luke Stephens wants to marry her because he loves her mind. Upon returning to her home and recognizing how much she has grown, Lyddie decides to defer marrying Luke until she has graduated from Oberlin. Her initial reasons for leaving home have come from a self-conscious recognition that she needs to learn how to earn a place in the world; her final decision is based on the epiphany that the only thing limiting her is her own self-image. She overcomes poverty, ignorance, and personal pettiness. She learns to balance her own materialism with her love of others and her love of learning.

Nevertheless, Paterson's *Bildungsroman* also fits Abel, Hirsch, and Langland's formulation in that Lyddie transfers her affections from intimacy with her family to intimacy with Luke — she is never emotionally autonomous — and her greatest lesson stems from her introspective recognition that she can define who she is. Her growth also adheres to Pratt's archetypal patterns: she is at her emotional strongest in the green world of her Vermont farm; there she is most likely to feel self-fulfilled. Moreover, her movement into the society of Lowell represents a curtailment of her freedom, but because this is a novel written for adolescents rather than adults, Lyddie achieves the type of transcendence Lissa Paul points out is far more common to children's than women's literature ("Enigma" 189). Most important, by novel's end, Lyddie is an adult, and she is as fully empowered as it is possible to imagine a woman of her social construction to be.[15] She has achieved the capacity to work and to love, defying Annis Pratt's suspicion that the female *Bildungsroman* is an impossibility. Barbara White notes that "the *Bildungsroman* concludes on an affirmative note" (13), a pattern in keeping with the traditions of children's and adolescent literature. *Lyddie* is also a romantic novel in a way that is common to many children's and adolescent novels because Paterson ultimately affirms the importance of the individual.

But Barbara White also points out that "many adolescent protagonists fail even to gain the knowledge or undergo the change of character required in the initiation story with its much looser definition" (13). Such novels are *Entwicklungsromane*, novels of development, that end before the protagonist reaches adulthood. Many of the YA novels that emerged in the 1970s that have subsequently been referred to as "problem novels" are *Entwicklungsromane*: the character grows as s/he faces and resolves one specific problem. But because the time span of the *Entwicklungsroman* is more truncated than that of the *Bildungsroman*, the protagonist of the problem novel is rarely an adult by the end of the narrative. Some adolescent novels even contain a major streak of anti-romanticism in the way that they fail to offer the possibility of achieving maturity as a form of redemption. A few of these *Entwicklungsromane* (some of Cormier's novels come immediately to mind) even go so far in denying the individual's importance within society that they are actually nihilistic. All but the bleakest of YA novels, however, affirm the adolescent's ability to grow at least a little. Characters in novels of development such as S. E. Hinton's *The Outsiders* or Walter Dean Myers's *Scorpions* (1988) grow, even if they have not achieved adulthood. In these novels, the protagonist experiences some form of conflict with authority and learns something about institutional accommodation within a family, a school, or a social group.

I think the reason so many people react negatively to a novel like *The Chocolate War* has something to do with the way they read it as failing to fulfill the obligation of the *Entwicklungsroman* to meet romantic expectations about growth. Anne Scott MacLeod, for instance, notes that Cormier's novels "violate the unwritten rule that fiction for the young, however sternly realistic the narrative material, must offer some portion of hope, must end at least with some affirmative message" (74). Anita Tarr has argued that "Cormier is irresponsible as a writer" for writing a novel that argues "all of reality is a sham, and that the entire world is evil and there is no use fighting it" ("Does" 7). MacLeod and Tarr may well imply that *The Chocolate War* fails as an adolescent novel because of their assumption that the genre requires *Bildung* of some sort. Romantic that I am, however, I still see redemption at the end of *The Chocolate War*. The book opens with the line "They murdered him," and much is made of crucifixion imagery in the second and the last chapters. In the second chapter, Obie recognizes the religious symbolism of the football field's goal posts: "The shadows of the goal posts sprawled on the field like grotesque crosses" (14). After being corrupted by Archie's insidious evil, Obie loses that recognition: "He looked at the goal posts. They reminded him of something. He couldn't remember" (190). Presumably, Obie no longer recognizes Christ and has lost the possibility of redemption. If Jerry has been crucified, it has been to expiate someone's sins. Goober, at least, has *seen* what has happened; I think Goober knows that Jerry has died for his sins. Whether Goober will gain anything by that recognition is a matter open to debate, but at least one character in this novel has been given the opportunity to grow. The reader has been offered that opportunity, too. In that potential growth lies whatever redemption the novel might offer. Thus, MacLeod and Tarr and I all agree on some implicit level that adolescent literature is at its heart a romantic literature because so many of us — authors, critics, teachers, teenagers — need to believe in the possibility of adolescent growth.

## Romanticism, Modernism, Postmodernism

When we identify a book as an *Entwicklungsroman* because the protagonist has grown or as a *Bildungsroman* because the protagonist reaches adulthood by the novel's end, we open ourselves to investigating the aesthetic philosophy that informs the text. We can identify *Lyddie* as a novel influenced by romanticism because of the way it affirms the individual or we can identify *The Chocolate War* as failing to meet the romantic expectations we have of the conventions of adolescent literature. But in both novels, the protagonist's growth is predicated on her or his ability to engage institutional power. Jerry Renault and Lyddie struggle economically. They struggle to communicate with other people, especially those who have authority over them. Both are anxious about their sexuality. Both must confront death. Both garner power by straining against repression. Foucault points out that power can be simultaneously repressive and enabling because those who are complacent are often less empowered than those who gain power by struggling (*History* 36–49; *Discipline* 195–228). Characters as divergent as Lyddie and Jerry Renault demonstrate empowerment within repression.

Foucault is the poststructural theorist who typifies social repression as having its roots in the discourses formed by social institutions to control people's powers: he is especially aware of the repression/power dynamic at work in how society regulates sexuality and the government.[16] Those two forces are certainly major ones in adolescent literature, so it seems to me that the tension between power and repression in adolescent novels may well be one of romanticism being reformed by postmodernism.[17] After all, the Young Adult novel as we know it came into being during the 1960s, well into the postmodern era. In other words, novels of development and of initiation — and for that matter, children's literature — evolved during a romantic era when many authors explored individual psychology, but the YA novel, with its questioning of social institutions and how they construct individuals, was not possible until the postmodern era influenced authors to explore what it means if we define people as socially constructed subjects rather than as self-contained individuals bound by their identities.

John McGowan considers romanticism, modernism, and post-modernism to be various stages of modernity, which he defines as the cultural condition in which society recognizes that it must "legitimate itself by its own self-generated principles, without appeal to external verities, authorities or traditions" (McGowan, *Postmodernism* 3). That is, modernity is the era in which humanity and its social organizations ceased to be consciously organized around principles dictated by religious faith. Modernity emerged in Western thinking around 1800 because of several interrelated factors, including Protestantism's challenges to Catholicism, increased industrialization, challenges to imperialism that led to a decreased sense of Eurocentrism, capitalism replacing feudalism as the chief principle of socioeconomic organization, and democracy's challenge to the divine rights of monarchy (McGowan, *Postmodernism* 3). One result of modernity was an increased interest in the novel of development, the *Entwicklungsroman*.

Romanticism was an early manifestation of society's effort in the era of modernity to self-legitimize that focuses on the individual's autonomy as liberating. Romanticism relies on a mythology that art is the means of legitimizing society. The artist's role is analogous to priesthood, and the cultural faith in transcendent individual growth represents an instance of society self-legitimizing (McGowan, *Postmodernism* 5–11). This faith in growth led to the specific development of the *Bildungsroman*. In the twentieth century, modernism refined modernity by focusing on "the heroic maintenance of the self" as providing an alternative to the depravity of humanity (McGowan, *Postmodernism* 11). Rather than art serving as a mythical justification for life, modernist art represents an antidote to the meaninglessness of capitalist society, according to McGowan ("Postmodernism" 585). The modernist artist is more monk than priest, a person who operates removed from society in order to achieve its greatest accomplishments.

Postmodernism, however, acknowledges the triumph of economics in determining a cultural self-legitimization. Postmodernism represents a socially self-conscious era of modernity in which the culture recognizes that some form of unity exists through the complete domination of capitalism over every aspect of social life (McGowan, *Postmodernism* 13). That is to say, if everything in culture is constituted by discourse and all discourse participates in the modes of production that enact society, then nothing escapes the capitalist institution. We are all subjects constituted by discourse, so we are all immersed irrevocably in capitalism. As Fredric Jameson would have it, postmodernism is "the cultural dominant of the logic of late capitalism" (Jameson, *Postmodernism* 46). The role of art in postmodernism then is to serve as a cultural practice that participates unavoidably in perpetuating capitalism (McGowan, "Postmodernism" 586). The postmodern artist contributes art to society as her or his means of production. And in some sense, maturity as transcendence has become impossible since so many of the markers of maturity are immersed in capitalism: driving, voting, buying liquor, obtaining a credit card, and paying income tax serve as typical rites of passage in postmodern culture. The Young Adult novel may well be the specific subgenre of the *Entwicklungsroman* — the novel of development — that has emerged from postmodern thinking. (This is not to imply that Young Adult novels *cannot* be *Bildungsromane*. *Lyddie*, for example, certainly is.) Young Adult novels are *Entwicklungsromane* or *Bildungsromane* that self-consciously explore the individual's power in relation to the institutions that comprise her or his existence. Thus, YA novels may or may not be *Bildungsromane*, depending more on the level of maturity the protagonist reaches than anything else.

*Entwicklungsromane* are projects of modernity in the way they participate in a mythology of cultural legitimization: our task as humans is to grow. In the romantic era, the *Bildungsroman* emerged from the *Entwicklungsroman* as a narrative of transcendence: the individual grows into an adulthood of autonomy and self-determination. In modernism, maturity often takes the form of a conscious rejection of society; separation, rather than transcendence, serves as the mark of the mature modernist. But postmodernism, cynical about the transformative power of maturity, marks growth largely in terms of the individual's increased participation in capitalism. The narrative of growth in postmodernism thus becomes constituted as an acceptance of one's cultural habitat rather than serving as a narrative about transcendence or separation. The postmodern awareness of the subject's inevitable construction as a product of language renders the construct of self-determination virtually obsolete. As a result, the popularity of the traditional *Bildungsroman* with its emphasis on self-determination gives way to the market dominance of the Young Adult novel, which is less concerned with depicting growth reverently than it is with investigating how the individual exists within society. Growth is possible in a postmodern world, especially if growth is defined as an increasing awareness of the institutions constructing the individual. But following World War II, maturity, adulthood, being harder to define, ceased to be privileged as the narrative goal in literature written for youth. The Young Adult novel, then, came into being as a genre precisely because it is a genre predicated on demonstrating characters' ability to grow into an acceptance of their environment. That is, the YA novel teaches adolescents how to exist within the (capitalistically bound) institutions that necessarily define teenagers' existence.

The YA novel allows for postmodern questions about authority, power, repression, and the nature of growth in ways that traditional *Bildungsromane* do not. Note that the *Bildungsroman* affords the protagonist slightly more social power at the end of the novel than an *Entwicklungsroman* does. Since most YA novels are *Entwicklungsromane* that end before the protagonist reaches adulthood, few of them depict their protagonists as fully enfranchised within their culture. In other words, *Bildungsromane* tend to allow for adolescents to overcome the condition of adolescence by becoming adults. As adults, they have relatively more social power than they had as adolescents. If we make the mistake of collapsing all adolescent literature into the rubric of the *Bildungsroman*, we miss the power differential between novels of development and coming-of-age novels. We also ignore the strain of romanticism that permeates the genre, but even worse, we elide the power structures at work in adolescent literature, rendering them virtually invisible. If we acknowledge the paradigm shift, however, we can perceive the relationship between the genre of the YA novel and the epistemological issues that engendered its emergence.

Ultimately, paying attention to the generic structures in adolescent narratives can help us classify literary patterns (that is, distinguishing *Bildungsromane* and *Entwicklungsromane*) and help us to identify the history of ideas working itself out in literature (recognizing the influences of romanticism, modernism, and postmodernism at work in a book). But more important, in recognizing how the generic characteristics that define the YA novel are both historically and aesthetically constructed, we can better analyze the entire genre. Much ink has been spilled over definitions of adolescent versus YA literature, but in my mind the real issue resides somewhere in the relationships between our romantic beliefs in growth, our postmodern awareness of the socially constructed limitations of power, and the adolescent's interactions with Ideological State Apparatuses as social institutions (such as how we construct sexuality, death, school, religion, gender, or family). Children's books are often about power and repression: Peter Rabbit, Max, and Ramona learn how to control their own personal power; Wilbur gains self-control over his fear of death. But the nature of power and repression that adolescents experience is far more outwardly focused, whether they develop as in an *Entwicklungsroman* or if they do achieve maturity, as in a *Bildungsroman*. And indeed, adolescents do not achieve maturity in a YA novel until they have reconciled themselves to the power entailed in the social institutions with which they must interact to survive.

I would submit that Young Adult literature has exploded as an institution in the postmodern era because although it affirms modernity's belief in the power of the individual implied by the very essence of the *Entwicklungsroman*, even more, it very self-consciously problematizes the relationship of the individual to the institutions that construct her or his subjectivity. The basic difference between a children's and an adolescent novel lies not so much in how the protagonist grows — even though the gradations of growth do help us better understand the nature of the genre — but with the very determined way that YA novels tend to interrogate social constructions, foregrounding the relationship between the society and the individual rather than focusing on Self and self-discovery as children's literature does.

### CHAPTER 2

# *"I don't know the words"*

INSTITUTIONAL DISCOURSES

IN ADOLESCENT LITERATURE

Avi's *Nothing but the Truth* ends with the statement, "I don't know the words" (177). *Nothing but the Truth* is a postmodern novel about a ninth-grader named Philip Malloy who gets expelled from Harrison High School for creating a disturbance during a broadcast over his school's public announcement system of "The Star-Spangled Banner" (177). His admitting that he does not know the words to the anthem provides an ironic twist to the story's resolution because his suspension has created a national media frenzy. Ostensibly, he has been suspended for trying to sing the national anthem during morning announcements in his homeroom. Local politicians have asserted the boy's right to salute his country, but Philip's teacher asserts that he was intentionally creating a disturbance because she recently gave him a failing grade that led to his suspension from the track team. During the course of events, she is forced to resign. Philip ultimately transfers to another school, where he finally admits that he has never known the lyrics to the national anthem.

His admission, "I don't know the words," serves as a metaphor for adolescents' position within many institutional cultures. Philip knows there are words — he knows that the language he needs to navigate within the institution exists — but he does not always have the capability of accessing those words. He is effectively silenced by three institutions that purport to empower people: school, family, and local government. Yet despite being denied full access to the language of institutional discourse, Philip has remarkable authority over his own destiny and the destiny of his teacher. He has access to the national media. He has access to the local school board. He can get a teacher fired. Yet he cannot communicate effectively enough with his own parents to stop the chain of events that follows when he first hums along during the broadcast of the national anthem. Foucault would note how Philip operates within a "domination-repression" model of institutional structure. The boy is invested in succeeding in the school — he wants to run track there — so he cares enough to test the limits of his power, but when he finds that limit, he is himself disempowered. If Philip loses in his institutional struggle, it is because he misperceives what power he has within the economy of his culture. His father, who claims to lack "a position of power" at work, urges his son, "Don't let them push you around" (56–57). As Philip tries to defend himself, one series of miscommunications builds upon another, demonstrating how institutions derive their power from the discourse people use.

Social institutions are determined by discourse, and they exist for the purpose of regulating social power, which is why Althusser refers to them as "Ideological State Apparatuses" (155). They use language simultaneously to repress and to empower their constituents; they gain power from the very people whom they regulate. As ISAs, social institutions also use language to regulate one another. In the case of the U.S. government, the Constitution designates three institutions to provide a system of checks and balances: the executive, legislative, and judicial branches of the government both sustain and regulate one another in a series of written and verbal interactions. Humans grow to maturity trained in the ways of such institutions; families, schools, and religious institutions all take an active role in educating children how to engage the institutional power afforded to individuals. The training invariably depends on language of some sort.

When we investigate how social institutions function in adolescent literature, we can gain insight into the ways that adolescent literature itself serves as a discourse of institutional socialization. Because institutions are myriad in number, I have chosen to focus on four that recur often in YA novels: government politics, schools, religion, and identity politics. As institutions with clearly defined goals of training children and adolescents, both schools and religion serve as sites of empowerment and repression for many adolescents. The role of politics in adolescent literature appears more subtly: relatively few novels deal directly with the role of the state in regulating teenagers' power. But many novels deal with this concept either metaphorically or by demonstrating the ways that teenagers are affected by government policies or are socially constructed by identity politics, including race, gender, and class. Virtually every adolescent novel assesses some aspect of the interaction between the individual adolescent and the institutions that shape her or him. When adolescent novels problematize institutions, they instinctively explore the issues of language in which the institution is immersed. Thus, as I interrogate how institutions interact with individuals in adolescent literature, I will also explore pertinent discursive issues. Novels about politics make manifest how ideology is a discursive construct. Novels set in schools demonstrate the paradoxical nature of the carnivalesque at work in literature. Novels that include religious topics foreground what it means for an institution to be comprised of competing voices, and novels that deal with identity politics demonstrate absence as a powerful discursive tool.

## Politics

According to Foucault, political institutions work because people give the ruler power. Modifying Rousseau's concept of the social contract, Foucault argues that "power has its principle not so much in a person as . . . in an arrangement whose internal mechanisms produce the relation in which individuals are caught up" (*Discipline* 202). He borrows the concept of the panopticon from Jeremy Bentham to demonstrate the power potential in an institution such as a prison. Bentham imagined the panopticon as the model of the perfect prison. He envisioned prison cells constructed in the shape of a wheel, with the interior walls open to the center of the circle. In that central point would be constructed a round watchtower from which guards could view all the cells at all times. Foucault argues that the possibility that prisoners were being watched would elicit their good behavior. In other words, Foucault asserts, the social contract with a state is not maintained so much by members of the society being watched by a constantly vigilant government as much as it is maintained by the members of the society *fearing* constant surveillance. They voluntarily give up any negative social behavior that might manifest itself as social control for fear of the state's reprisal.

Yoshida Junko has argued that this model shapes the social structure of the school in Cormier's *The Chocolate War*. Defining The Vigils as the watchtower and Trinity as the prison they regulate, Yoshida demonstrates how the adolescents at Trinity willingly cede their power to their perceived dominators in order to escape possible punishment (110–112). As a result, The Vigils have complete control of Trinity, even usurping the authority of their schoolmasters. In that sense, *The Chocolate War* is the same sort of dark adolescent fantasy that *Lord of the Flies* is: when adolescents achieve total control, they become totally corrupt. Both novels are metaphors for the concept that absolute power corrupts absolutely.

Many critics have metaphorical interpretations for the politics at work in *The Chocolate War*. Anne Scott MacLeod argues that what happens at Trinity is a microcosmic metaphor for American politics (75), while Perry Nodelman interprets the chocolate war as a metaphor for the Vietnam War (Nodelman, "Robert Cormier" 102). Jan Susina interprets The Vigils as the Mafia (171), and Cormier himself has identified big business as the central metaphor of the novel (DeLuca and Natov 119). At the heart of all these interpretations is the recognition that *The Chocolate War* is a political novel. It is an investigation of social organization and how individuals interact with that organization. The novel communicates that institutions are more powerful than individuals, but that individuals who engage their own power can affect the shape of the institution. Cormier implies that as social organizations, institutions are not to be trusted.

Few adolescent novels are as direct as Cormier's are in addressing government as a form of social organization, although almost all adolescent novels are informed by ideologies that are political in nature. That is, all novels are influenced by their authors' sociopolitical beliefs. Basing his arguments on the work of Althusser, Peter Hollindale notes that ideology is not "a political policy, . . . it is a climate of belief" ("Ideology" 19). As I tell my students, we believe some ideologies so deeply that we consider them Truth: such ideologies as "education can improve people's lives" and "it's better to be rich than poor" can be difficult for people brought up in capitalist societies to recognize as arguable positions.[1] But all adolescent novels are informed by such sociopolitical beliefs.

Laura Ingalls Wilder, for example, infuses her own libertarian ideologies into all of the Little House books, but most especially into the later books written for adolescents. Although in actuality the Ingalls family was closely connected to their neighbors during the historical season of blizzards depicted in *The Long Winter* (1940), Wilder portrays the fictionalized Ingalls family as living entirely isolated in self-sufficiency. Influenced by libertarianism, her ideological goal was to portray government intervention as both unnecessary and suspicious (Fellman 101–116). William Sleator's *House of Stairs* (1974), Robert Cormier's *I Am the Cheese* (1977), and Virginia Hamilton's *The Gathering* (1981) provide similar ideological critiques of government politics.

William Sleator's disturbing science fiction novel *House of Stairs* bears all the ideological marks of the 1970s post–Vietnam era's fears. In Sleator's novel, the government funds a research study on the possibility of using operant conditioning to alter the behavior of five orphaned teenagers. They are isolated in a horrific institution, a structure filled with nothing but stairs. The five parentless adolescents engage in endless power struggles with each other and with the machine that supplies their food. Three of the teenagers, Blossom, Oliver, and Abigail, are particularly adroit at manipulating the situation because they rely on traditional gender roles to do so. The two more androgynous characters, Peter and Lola, resist repression and are eventually able to escape the evils of the government's efforts to condition them, although the price they pay is a harrowing emotional toll. The reader can deduce several political ideologies from *House of Stairs*: fear institutions; fear the government; fear those who rely on traditional gender roles to gain power; and trust that resistance leads to empowerment. This last ideology makes the novel particularly nuanced because it does not shy away from depicting both the good and the bad of the dynamic between power and repression that informs so many teenagers' lives. They may rebel against institutions, but the rebellion will come at a cost.

Cormier's *I Am the Cheese* is an even more assertive indictment of the American government as an institution. The protagonist's family participates in the federal government's witness protection program because his father is a journalist who needs protection from organized crime. The family's new name is "Farmer," the protagonist becomes "Adam" because he is the first Farmer. Mr. Farmer teases his son, singing "The Farmer in the Dell" to him to emphasize the interrelationship of the members of their family. But when the federal agent charged with protecting the family turns on them and Mr. Farmer and his wife are killed, Adam enters the government's so-called protective custody and becomes subject to mind control in an effort to erase his knowledge that the government played a role in killing his parents. Adam defines himself as the cheese who stands alone in an ironic interplay of discourses between children's culture and political culture. The nursery rhyme "The Farmer in the Dell" describes aptly his political situation.

His incarceration and subsequent interrogation are defined in terms of the tension between children's culture and adult political culture. Like a child, his language is limited because he ostensibly suffers from amnesia and does not have the words to connect his present condition to his past. Like the protagonist of *Nothing but the Truth*, Adam does not know the words he needs to know to escape his current situation. But as he gains access to language and enters into discourse with the adult agent of the U.S. government, Adam regains partial memories, so his knowledge appears to be increasing. The agent interrogating him encourages the boy to reveal what he remembers about his past, but Adam's refusal to do so probably saves his life, since the agent will surely kill him if he reveals having any knowledge of his father's murder. The agent eventually recommends that the government either kill Adam or drug him into total amnesia, so the betrayal of Adam's trust is complete. The novel is thus a cynical commentary on post-Watergate American politics: Because Adam has been betrayed by a government he once thought benevolent, he becomes paranoid of the government having too much power, just as Cormier implies many Americans feel betrayed by the government and therefore paranoid about government control. If Adam lives in a panopticon of government agents and medical personnel trying to elicit information from him before they "terminate" him, so perhaps do we all.

It is significant that the currency in the interaction between the individual and government as an institution in *I Am the Cheese* is language. The dynamic between Adam's memory and his ability to articulate narratives about his past is a fluid one: he appears at once powerless while he cannot remember the words to describe his past and powerful because the government is so interested in his loss of memory. As he gains access to language, he develops the power to intimidate the government agent — but if Adam reveals too many of his memories, he will become completely powerless because he will be killed. As long as Adam can control his utterances, he can control his position within the government. He may appear to be passive; he may appear to be a victim; but he still has enough power in this situation that his life has some value to the government, so he remains alive. Access to discourse both endangers Adam and saves him from the American government. Interestingly, as long as he is caught in this dynamic, he cannot become an adult. We can measure his power by the fact that his story could never be classified as a *Bildungsroman*.

Although most adolescent novels are not this directly involved in political commentary, they invariably reflect some cultural biases, most of which are likely to be veiled in ideological discourses that affirm widely held societal views. Avi's *Nothing but the Truth* affirms the importance of education, for example; Harper Lee's *To Kill a Mockingbird* (1960) condemns racism. When ideologies in YA novels focus specifically on government, they tend to convey to adolescents that they are better served by accepting than by rejecting the social institutions with which they must live. In that sense, the underlying agenda of many YA novels is to indoctrinate adolescents into a measure of social acceptance.

Virginia Hamilton's *The Gathering* is one such political novel. The story is the third book of the *Justice* trilogy in which four telepathic children travel into the future to affect a positive change for the dystopia they find there. Their development hinges on their belief that they have the power to improve the world. Justice is the leader of "the unit," as they call themselves collectively; her twin brothers, Thomas and Levi, and their friend Dorian work with her to create this telepathic unit. They call the dystopia of Earth's future "Dustland." The primitive cultures they find there fight to sustain life in a world filled with dust that has resulted from thermonuclear accidents, war, and natural disasters. The planet is populated with a number of mutants, implying that the war has been a nuclear war. Eventually, Justice and the unit discover that several "domities" exist on the planet. These are computer-controlled cities built under domes where species are preserved and everyone is happy . . . because the computer that regulates the climate infuses sedatives into the air.

Reminiscent of Hal in Stanley Kubrick's *2001: A Space Odyssey*, the computer called "Colossus" has too much power. Unlike Hal, however, Colossus has rejected its own evil. That evil transforms itself into a distinct entity that calls itself "Mal." Mal is a Lucifer figure ejected from paradise who takes it upon itself to banish any nonconformist creature from the domity into the hell of Dustland: "Mal must have order and sameness" (124). Justice and the unit discover that although nonconformity is not tolerated in the domity, the rebels who live in Dustland have become stronger, hardier people for having endured adversity. The unit eventually destroys Mal so that the Colossus becomes capable of accepting difference and integrating it into life in the domity. That a group working as a whole defeats a tyrant creates a typical American commentary on political structures: democracies are preferable to single rulers.

Several of the book's other ideologies surface as political beliefs shared by many Americans. The book is a proenvironmentalism, antiwar narrative that participates in the ongoing dialogue about nuclear proliferation during the Cold War in the same way that Sylvia Engdahl's *Enchantress from the Stars* (1970) and Madeleine L'Engle's *A Swiftly Tilting Planet* (1978) do. *The Gathering* also promotes a positive ideology involving racial pride because Justice and the unit are accomplished black children who are clearly positioned as the saviors of their world and of the future. Moreover, the scene when they lead the rebels through the underground passage in Dustland to the domity reads much like a tale about the Underground Railroad, Moses leading his people out of Egypt, or like a reverse journey of the Middle Passage.

> Slakers, whose myth was that they would never again go beneath the dust, were outraged at going under.
> Still, all who were left of the gathering went under. Dust rose on both sides. They could not see ahead of them. They hurried.

There was no darkness, some sickness, but again they could not see in front of them. They passed through indescribable color beyond the light spectrum they knew.

It is a divide, spoke the unit to itself. It is what separates Dustland from what really is beyond it. The color divide is the final barrier to another place. (63)

Color (wrongly) separates these people, just as perceptions of racial color wrongly separate people in America. Once the refugees from Dustland are inside the domity, Thomas points out that different species in the city are separated from one another in a social grouping he identifies as segregation (76). Hamilton is relying on the reader's knowledge of history to impart the antislavery ideology embedded in the text. Her allusion to the Middle Passage is not overt. But the ideology of antiracism is indeed direct. Hamilton expects her readers to consider segregation evil. Moreover, Hamilton links race and gender when the android who serves as the unit's tour guide is bemused at the children's tendency to segregate themselves by gender (83). Mal, after all, has banished another species that relies on distinct genders because "all must be the same here" (125). Gender difference is not tolerated in this culture, but species do not intermingle, either.

These elements add up to create a story about the necessity and beauty of diversity. Written at the beginning of the Reagan era, at a time when the advances made by the Civil Rights movement had begun to be ignored, when preppies were prevalent and the concept of "yuppies" was born, when the Religious Right had gathered more strength than it had had in America since the 1920s, and when a feminist backlash had begun to take place, *The Gathering* demonstrates what happens when an entire culture requires itself to look alike or think alike. No one is unhappy, but no one is completely happy, either. People are drugged and mindless. To demonstrate the problem with this model of conformity, Hamilton employs a music metaphor. One Dustlander the children bring into the domity cannot conform to the group he is assigned. He is maladjusted because he thinks that the song he is supposed to sing in harmony with his group is tedious compared to the songs he sang in his former life, when he was leader of both the hunt and the song in the dust outside of the domity.

Singing together can be empowering, but not if the group is limited to only one song.

*The Gathering* links conformity to issues of power. Twice, the android in charge of the domity tells the children a rationalization for control that sounds compatible with Nazism: "We control for the efficiency of the result" (79) and "there is efficiency in control" (109). The computer Colossus and its alter ego Mal have complete power over all inhabitants of Dustland and its domities, so they are the only institution of significance in this culture. Hamilton makes clear that any institution with absolute power is ultimately untenable for several reasons, but mostly because "nothing, no one is perfect," as Justice puts it (116). Humans have created the supercomputer that rules Dustland, so it, too, is fallible as the machine's expectations that humans can live without diversity or without conflict eventually demonstrates. The computer's efforts to eliminate conflict — well intentioned as they originally are — result in the dehumanization of humanity.

In promoting the tolerance of diversity, *The Gathering* extols the virtues of nonconformity that occur within the social contract. Thomas, the book's rebel, loses his lifelong stutter only when he finally rejects the jealousy and anger that have dominated his life. As the doppelgänger of his twin brother, Levi, Thomas is the evil twin, the dark twin. He overcomes his malevolence so that he can exist in the world peacefully. He still plays his kettledrums, violating the mores of a typical teenager in small-town Ohio, but since this nonconformism hurts no one, the social institutions within which he exists tolerate the behavior. His destructive temper, however, is extinguished, implying to the reader a difference between constructive and destructive rebellion. It is only after having witnessed an all-powerful institution that Thomas recognizes as corrupt that he can give up his own pretensions to complete domination of other people. He accepts his place in the social contract only after having tried to violate it and after having witnessed the results of a large-scale violation of the social contract perpetrated by the supercomputer that regulates humanity in the domity. Most significant, the metaphor for his acceptance of the power that institutions have over him is a discursive one: when he does not accept his role in any domination-repression model institution, he cannot participate in his culture's discourse because of his stutter. When he accepts the limitations institutions place on him, he becomes discursively fluent. He can speak without stuttering.

In order to understand the political ideologies at work in books like *The Long Winter*, *I Am the Cheese*, or *The Gathering*, the reader has to understand at least two things: the historical context in which the story is set and the historical context in which it was written. The distinction is especially important for historical novels like *The Long Winter*, when the historical setting is significantly removed from the date of the novel's publication. As Fredric Jameson puts it, "Always historicize!" (*Political Unconscious* 9). Analyses of ideology within historical context help determine the "particular forms of signification which play a particular political role in particular historical societies" (Bennett 146). Readings that ignore context to emphasize "some universal, invariant form of cognition to which there is attributed an invariant political effect" result in "aesthetic" readings that are necessarily incomplete (146).

Investigations of political discourse at work in adolescent fiction often occur in history classes: historians frequently teach Baum's *The Wonderful Wizard of Oz* (1900) as a parable of populism.[2] The Colliers' *My Brother Sam Is Dead* (1974) and Esther Forbes's *Johnny Tremain* (1943) are often taught in conjunction with American history classes. But it is not enough to use novels to teach about the historical period in which they are set. These novels are themselves historical artifacts of the time period during which they were written, so *My Brother Sam Is Dead* imparts anti-Vietnam sentiment whereas *Johnny Tremain* questions American involvement in World War II. And these novels deal with the place of the individual in relation to the government as a political institution. All of them grapple with the individual's relationship to the institution in terms of power and control, and all of them imply that the individual is inevitably affected by her or his institutional affiliations.

## School

The concept of school as a social institution is omnipresent in adolescent literature. The classic *Bildungsroman* describes the protagonist's education, and many *Entwicklungsromane* are set in school environments. Beverly Lyon Clark defines a specific subset of adolescent literature, the traditional School Story, as a story set at a school (usually a boarding school) that is addressed to children from the point of view of a child. The text is usually middle-class in its perspective (Clark 3). If the canonical boys' version of these books can be said to have a formula, it is this: they cover a broad range of years, from an ordinary boy's arrival at the school through his years of service to older boys until he is himself one of the older boys at the school. Two types of adventures occur: competition at physical activities, such as sports, and some sort of social conflict that allows the text to explore morality. The tale may conclude with an affirmation of the school's purpose in training young people to take their place in the status quo of the social order (Clark 4). Certainly girls' school stories serve the same ideological purpose, which is the most important purpose of School Stories; their agenda to indoctrinate children into the social order is thinly veiled.[3]

Since American YA novels are usually *Entwicklungsroman*, they are far more likely to focus on one set of problems than they are to show a character developing over a period of time as School Stories generally do. But although the time line of the plot may be telescoped, the function of the narrative remains the same: school serves as an institutional setting in which the protagonist can learn to accept her or his role as a member of other institutions. M. E. Kerr's *Is That You, Miss Blue?* (1975) demonstrates the fusion of the School Story and the problem novel. Flanders Brown is a sophomore sent to boarding school at the class-conscious Charles School, an Episcopal school for girls in Virginia. Flanders's parents are recently divorced because her mother left her father in search of an identity independent of his. Flanders's "problem" is that she feels unwanted; her feelings of rejection are exacerbated because her mother is sleeping with a younger man and her father is exposed on national television as a charlatan who dabbles in sex therapy as a form of religion. But in watching the Charles School use its institutional power to persecute Miss Blue, one of the teachers who is a religious fanatic, Flanders gains the empathy she needs to forgive her parents. Her crisis and resolution occur during the course of a semester rather than over the course of several years, as would be traditional in a School Story. But as an *Entwicklungsroman, Is That You, Miss Blue?* affirms the possibility of individual growth within a corrupt culture without taking that individual all the way to adulthood. Nevertheless, the book demonstrates how in rejecting one institution — the Charles School — an adolescent like Flanders can eventually embrace the institutions that are vital for her continued growth: in this case, the institution of family.

*Is That You, Miss Blue?* also typifies how schools function as institutions in YA literature. School serves as the metaphorical representation of the many institutions that will influence adolescents throughout their lives. Kerr even beats the reader over the head with the school-as-microcosm motif when she writes, "Boarding school is like a little world, with all the lessons of the large one taught in minuscule" (168). School settings exist in adolescent literature to socialize teenagers into accepting the inevitable power social institutions have over individuals in every aspect of their lives. Some YA novels are sanguine about this process; others are cynical, but if these novels have an element that purports to empower teenagers, that sense of uplift is often balanced by the acknowledgment that although social institutions give in adolescent literature, they also take away.

The schools in Daniel Pinkwater's stories demonstrate this phenomenon nicely. In *Alan Mendelsohn, the Boy from Mars* (1979), Leonard Neeble meets Alan at their school, Bat Masterson. That Pinkwater has named his school with an approximate anagram of the word "masturbation" conveys the book's jovial lack of respect for school as an institution. Yet it is the discipline meted out to them by this institution (when Alan is suspended and Leonard is given a psychological leave of absence) that frees them to have a set of adventures that includes interplanetary communication and telepathic journeys to another plane of existence. The boys have rebelled at Bat Masterson and so must be institutionally repressed, but they, ironically, transform the repression into far greater empowerment than they had previously had. Most significantly, after Alan returns to live in his hometown on Mars, Leonard adopts a new set of friends and learns to navigate the social culture of Bat Masterson. He still periodically rebels by intimidating his teachers with his advanced knowledge, but he does so within parameters acceptable to them. After all, as Leonard puts it, "There's a gentle art to bugging teachers. You have to sort of pace yourself, or you'll spoil it" (245). The same can be said of pushing any institutional boundary.

The dynamic of (over)regulation → unacceptable rebellion → repression → acceptable rebellion → transcendence-within-accepted-limits is a common one in YA novels set at schools. All of Leonard Neeble and Alan Mendelsohn's "astromental" escapades in *Alan Mendelsohn, the Boy from Mars* result from the boys' rebellion against their school. The adolescent characters in *Is That You, Miss Blue?* rebel against the merged institutions of church and school at the Charles School before they make peace with their parents. Holden Caulfield rebels against Pencey Prep before he accepts the larger society he once rejected as phony. A book radically different from Kerr's and Pinkwater's and Salinger's, Wilder's *The Little Town on the Prairie* (1941), even exhibits this pattern. Only after the children rebel against Miss Wilder's inappropriate use of discipline does Laura become herself empowered to serve as a teacher. Adolescents have to fail at one form of institutionally proscribed rebellion before they find an institutionally tolerated form of rebellion that paradoxically allows them to remain within the system.

The paradox of rebelling to conform sets up enough ironic tension that subversiveness against school authorities becomes a source of humor in many YA novels. In Sue Townsend's *The Secret Diary of Adrian Mole, Aged 13 ¾* (1982), for example, the headmaster of Adrian's school calls the entire school to an assembly:

> Mr. Scruton got up on the stage and acted like the films of Hitler. He said in all his long years of teaching he had never come across an act of such serious vandalism. Everybody went dead quiet and wondered what had happened. Scruton said that somebody had entered his office and drawn a mustache on Margaret Thatcher and written "Three million unemployed" in her cleavage. He said that defiling the greatest leader this country has ever known was a crime against humanity. (172)

That the vandal proves to have been a teacher makes the subversiveness all the more successful from the narrator's point of view. In another comic novel, Paul Zindel's *The Pigman* (1968), John details how to detonate firecrackers in the bathroom at schools and outlines how to orchestrate an entire class in a timed activity called a "supercolossal fruit roll" designed to terrify substitute teachers (2). The subversiveness stays with teenagers long after the plot does: my husband remembers nothing about *The Pigman* except how to bomb a bathroom, and I modified the supercolossal fruit roll quite effectively when I was a junior in high school. Perhaps that behavior even served to empower me because subsequent teachers were terrified of our class. If Freud is right that the purpose of humor is to release people from their feelings of social restraint, then much of the antiestablishment humor pitched against school authorities in YA literature is right on the mark.[4] As David Russell notes, "comedy represents a rebellion against rules imposed by society" (118).

Rebelling against school authorities often serves the same function in adolescent literature that carnivals played in medieval Europe. According to Bakhtin, carnivals were:

> Sharply distinct from the serious official, ecclesiastical, feudal, and political cult forms and ceremonials. They offered a completely different, nonofficial, extraecclesiastical and extrapolitical aspect of the world, of man, and of human relations; they built a second world and a second life outside officialdom, a world in which all medieval people participated more or less. ("Rabelais and His World" 197)

John Stephens notes how often the carnivalesque in children's (and adolescent) literature teaches children to question the social order (120–121).[5] Much of the humor and virtually all of the rebellion in adolescent novels about school rely on carnivalesque departures from the status quo to lull the adolescent into eventually embracing it. By providing for an emotional outlet, antiestablishment humor helps teenagers reconcile themselves to living with the establishment.

Understandably, teenagers experience school as a site in which they are simultaneously repressed by authority and peers and in which they are liberated by socializing with their friends and by learning new ideas. Adolescent characters from Amy March to Weetzie Bat enjoy learning in an environment with other teenagers even while they detest the repression they experience at the hands of their teachers. Only once they rebel against authoritarian representatives of the institution are they able to grow. Gene Forrester and his friend Phineas, for example, define freedom as rejecting the strictures of their school in *A Separate Peace*. The narrator explains that "Phineas didn't really dislike West Point in particular or authority in general, but just considered authority the necessary evil against which happiness was achieved by reaction, the backboard which returned all the insults he threw at it" (10). Without rules, Phineas would have no raison d'être, because "Finny's life was ruled by inspiration and anarchy, and so he prized a set of rules" (25). The boys are empowered by breaking the rules, but when during one of their pranks Finny falls from a tree, breaking his leg badly enough that he is crippled, Gene begins to understand the purpose of rules: "If you broke the rules, then they broke you" (61–62).

Gene carries a burden of guilt because jealousy for Finny's achievement led him to bounce on the tree branch in the first place. Gene has caused his best friend's fall. His feelings of responsibility intensify after Finny breaks his leg a second time and dies during the corrective surgery. Gene recognizes that his own inner turmoil has caused evil; he achieves maturity only when he accepts that the enemy that needs quenching is the enemy within. His own unruly nature is the enemy, not the institution against which he has been rebelling. He has achieved the Victorian spiritual enlightenment that is foundational in the *Bildungsroman* as a genre. A Freudian might argue that Gene's superego has learned to regulate his id, or a Bakhtinian might say that the pressure-letting function of the adolescent's carnivalesque actions has served its purpose. Either way, Gene has internalized the necessary message: rebellion is good to a point. It helps adolescents release pent-up energies, perhaps even prevents worse disruptions of the social order. But the rebellion is only portrayed as effective in literature as long as it ultimately serves to sustain the status quo at some level. If rebellion goes uncontained, it becomes problematic. Thus, Gene conforms to the expectations his culture places on him. Gene has felt restricted, has rebelled, has faced terrible consequences, and is ironically most empowered when he finally embraces the very restrictions he rejected in the first place. Gene as an adult narrates his *Bildungsroman*, so we know he has grown to accept his place in society. As an adult, he seems to exist within his culture far more functionally than he did as an adolescent.

*The Chocolate War* takes that theme one step further. Jerry tries to stand up to corruption at his school and is effectively killed for his efforts. As Brother Leon and Archie, leader of The Vigils, struggle to assert their power over one another, the reader gradually begins to realize that it does not matter which of them controls the school, since they are two sides of the same coin. They collude in the ultimate punishment of Jerry because they are both individuals who mistake the power they have within an institution for individual power. Archie celebrates his own power over The Vigils as an organization (30, 168); then he rejoices at how "powerful the organization had become" (55). Archie expresses his power in a discourse shaped by sexual language, "Archie alone was always under pressure, devising the assignments, working them out. As if he was some kind of machine. Press a button: out comes an assignment. What did they know about the agonies of it all? The nights he tossed and turned? The times he felt used up, empty?" (30). Patricia Campbell makes note of a scene Cormier omitted from the final version of the novel in which Archie, impotent in the face of Jerry's defiance, achieves masturbatory climax after he devises a plan by which he can control Jerry (Campbell 41). Archie and Brother Leon are enmeshed in a homoerotic triangle: first the chocolate sale, then Jerry Renault serve as the object of exchange between the two men. The culmination of their relationship occurs as they watch Jerry's broken body carried away in an ambulance after the melee of the boxing match, an adolescent carnival if ever there was one. Brother Leon then puts his arm around Archie to shield him from another teacher's wrath, "And Archie realized that Leon was still in command, still in the position of power" (188). The avenging teacher stalks off. "Archie and Leon watched him go. Archie smiled inside. But he masked his feelings. Leon was on his side. Beautiful. Leon and The Vigils and Archie. What a great year it was going to be" (189). Archie has rebelled and been rewarded in a triumph of the carnivalesque. The open alliance between the two forces of evil in the school is made more menacing by the implied homophobia in Cormier's text: the reader is meant to despise these two males who are so corrupt that they have reached the ostensible pinnacle of debauchery, homosexuality.

Despite the insidious homophobia that infuses *The Chocolate War*, Cormier intends adolescents to understand that it is their moral obligation to disturb the universe, to rage and fight against the Archies and the Leons of the world lest the dark forces of the carnival gain too much power. The reader, then, must serve as the J. Alfred Prufrock of this text: s/he must decide whether to disturb the universe. Jerry's defeat challenges adolescent readers to temporarily destroy the social order so that it may ultimately be preserved.

## Religion

*The Chocolate War* and *Is That You, Miss Blue?* involve the intersection of school and religion as institutions, since both books are set at church schools. Adolescent novels that deal with religion as an institution demonstrate how discursive institutions are and how inseparable religion is from adolescents' affiliation with their parents' identity politics. Adolescents in such novels eventually experience language determining not only their religious beliefs, but also creating competing dialogues that influence their own religious views. Moreover, such novels depict how religion influences identity politics, especially those of race, class, and gender. Chaim Potok's *The Chosen* (1967), Laurence Yep's *Dragonwings* (1975), and M. E. Kerr's *What I Really Think of You* (1982) all interrogate the interaction between discourse and teenagers' sense of their identities in relation to their perceptions of their parents' identities. And all of the protagonists in these novels experience some form of the (over)regulation → unacceptable rebellion → repression → acceptable rebellion → transcendence model that typifies the domination-repression model of institutional discourse common in adolescent literature.

Reuven Malter narrates the story of his friendship with the considerably repressed Daniel Saunders in Potok's *The Chosen*, beginning with their first meeting in 1944 when they are fifteen and

continuing until they graduate from college. Reuven and Danny
are both Jewish boys living in New York, although Danny's family
is far more conservative than Reuven's, since Danny's father is a
Hasidic rabbi. Danny is expected to become his community's next
rabbi. Much of the story involves Danny's tense relationship with
his father and how the boy eventually fulfills a different destiny
than the one his father has chosen for him. But initially, Danny
and Reuven identify completely with the roles their fathers expect
them to play. Danny wears the earlocks and traditional garb worn
by the Hasidic community; Reuven wears the prayer shawl and
yarmulke his father expects him to wear. Reuven is a Zionist like
his father; Danny supports the anti-Zionist movement that his
father promotes, even though the boy is personally sympathetic
to the establishment of a Jewish national state. Both boys adhere
to their fathers' diets, and neither questions the legitimacy of the
Ten Commandments that are the foundation of their faith. Both
boys are comfortable with the complete dominance of male voices
in their families: Reuven's mother is dead, and Danny's mother
has a chronic illness that makes her little more than a shadow in
the plot. For both boys, God is entirely masculine. In this novel,
as in many about religious beliefs, religion becomes a matter of
personal identity; whole communities of Jews define themselves
entirely in terms of their religious identity. And that identity is
determined solely by patriarchs.

Reuven's relationship with his father serves as a foil to Danny's
relationship to his father. Reuven's father is a professor, so he
wants his son to become a professor. Yet because the two have
such a close relationship, Professor Malter readily accepts his son's
decision to become a rabbi. Professor Malter fervently believes
that because of the Holocaust, America needs more rabbis to re-
build Judaism, so he sanctions his son's choice. Reb Saunders
eventually blesses his son Daniel's decision to become a psycholo-
gist, but only after he has subjected his son to more than a decade
of a silent treatment devised to teach his son compassion. "The
heart speaks through silence," he explains to his son the day they
finally discuss Daniel's refusal to become a rabbi (265). Reuven
has described the silence as "weird" (191) and "bizarre" (209); it
seems unnatural to him that a man so language-oriented that he

will spend hours debating the meaning of one scriptural passage would refuse to allow any emotional discourse to take place between him and his son.

When contrasted with the many competing voices in the novel, Reb Saunders's silence with his son seems especially profound, but it also helps to explain the discursive nature of Judaism. Informed by the Torah, the Talmud, and its commentators; expressed in lengthy prayers and myriad chants and songs; factionalized by many schisms and political debates, Judaism as it is depicted in *The Chosen* is a religion determined entirely by language as an attempt to capture the ineffable spark of God that exists within each person (263). The religion itself demonstrates Bakhtin's concept of heteroglossia: competing voices interact with one another, influencing the shape of the whole (*Dialogic Imagination* 269–275). The Jews in this story engage in intricate and contentious interrogations of holy scripture and endless debates about its interpretation as a way to demonstrate God's presence in their lives, but they are unified in their grief for the six million Jews murdered in the Holocaust. Within the narrative itself, Hasidic Jews and the Orthodox Jews they call "apikoros" (meaning "sinners") compete for the dominant dialogue that will define what it means to be Jewish. Their competing voices, in turn, determine the dialogic nature of *The Chosen*, for it is a novel filled with competing dialogues. In one instance of the type of meticulous discourse that informs Judaism for Reuven, he spends four three-hour class periods explicating nine lines of the Talmud in one of his college classes that includes Jews who are both Hasidic and Orthodox. When he has completed his explanation, his professor asks him an unanticipated question that no one, including Reuven, can answer. After a lengthy silence, the professor tells him, "no one can explain it. . . . The truth is, I cannot explain it myself. . . . A teacher can also sometimes not know" (236). The narrative implies that if there is only one thing Jews can agree on, it is that discourse is ultimately inadequate to explain God fully.

Reb Saunders, however, has employed a different tack from the discourse-rich culture that surrounds him: he has been virtually silent with his son, ostensibly to teach him compassion. The rabbi's exercise in noncommunication seems to have achieved its purpose, for his son is indeed compassionate when he graduates from college. Danny even concedes that the terrible price he has paid in not having an emotional relationship with his father may have been worthwhile when he admits to Reuven's father that if necessary, he will follow the same child-rearing methods with his own son. For a young adult obsessed with language — he has taught himself German so that he can read Freud in the original — the concession seems a startling one, until the reader recognizes that Reb Saunders's actions have replicated God's to some degree. A believer may be surrounded by religious discourse, but few people actually experience the direct spoken word of God expressed to them individually. Believers are like Danny: they know God's love exists, just as the boy knows his father loves him, even if it is not expressed in direct personal discourse. *The Chosen* implies that we are all Daniels, surrounded by human discourse but still living necessarily in the silence, the aporia — the gap of unknowability — that results from our inability to engage in dialogue with the supreme deity. *The Chosen* thus constructs patriarchal silence in metaphorical contrast to discursive conflict as a way to communicate the final authority of that-which-lies-beyond-discourse. Poststructural thinking may not allow for any institution to exist outside of language, but Chaim Potok's *The Chosen* does. As Naomi Wood notes, "religion in children's literature functions as a mechanism of social ordering" (1). Children and adolescents taught to believe in the omnipotence of an unseen patriarchal deity who must be obeyed are indeed receiving ideological training that represses them.

Just as various forms of Judaism compete to form the discourse of *The Chosen*, various aspects of Chinese theology compete to influence the protagonist of Laurence Yep's *Dragonwings*. When he arrives in America in 1903, Moonshadow is an eight-year-old Chinese immigrant. His father belongs to the Company of the Peach Orchard Vow, a collaborative group of men whose religion is traditional Chinese ancestor worship, although one member of the company is Buddhist (23). The leader of their group refers to their home as "a superior home for superior men"; he is "fond of the phrase "the superior man," which he has borrowed from Confucian philosophy (21). Moonshadow and his father, Windrider, believe in reincarnation and practice filial piety; they make tributes to the Stove King to honor the Jade Emperor, the Lord of

Heaven and Earth. Weimen Mo and Wenju Shen describe the repression of children at work in Chinese children's literature that advances ideologies of filial piety; their work makes manifest the ethics of "subservience and humiliating sacrifice" required of child characters who practice filial piety faithfully (22). In *Dragonwings*, Moonshadow is subservient to his father, Windrider, who believes himself to be the reincarnation of a dragon. He believes this because in a vision, the Dragon King has told Windrider that in his former life, he was "the greatest physician of all the dragons" (38). Windrider believes that in this life, he must repent of his former pride. Only by learning to live humbly and serve others can he regain his status as a dragon. Windrider decides to atone for his sins by learning to fly, and his son's needs become secondary to his own.

Windrider experiences a number of competing discourses, not least of which is the complete disdain of the members of his company for his spirituality. None of the company of the Peach Orchard Vow is willing to believe that the Dragon King has spoken to Windrider. Mocking him, they dismiss the vision as a dream. How the reader interprets the conflict between Windrider and his friends even positions the reader in the middle of competing dialogues about the book's genre. If the members of the company are right and Windrider has dreamed his conversation with the Dragon King, the book is completely realistic, that is, the events in the book are probable. But if Windrider has indeed had a vision, the book is actually a fantasy: it is not feasible in the tangible world as we know it.

Yet another competing dialogue comes from Windrider's sense of duty to his wife and son. Building a flying machine saps his family's resources so that they must live in poverty while he proves himself. With information he learns from the Wright brothers, he builds an aeroplane and flies for a few moments. In the ensuing crash, however, he decides that "there's more to being a dragon than just flying. . . . Dragons have immense families too. . . . And it may be that my final test is to raise a brood of superior women and men" (242). Windrider's decision to synthesize the competing dialogues of living a pious life and supporting a family into a spiritual life that includes both makes it easier for the Company of the Peach Orchard Vow to resolve their differences with Windrider. In the end, although Moon-shadow develops in a growth pattern typical of an *Entwicklungsro-man*, Windrider's growth is the more dramatic growth of the *Bil-dungsroman*, for he experiences the education, the spiritual growth, and the ability to balance work and love that are common to that genre. That Yep demonstrates an adult experiencing competing institutional dialogues as he grows to maturity is an unusual but laudatory strategy in an adolescent novel. But for Moonshadow, spirituality is a matter of both sacrifice and reward, of both en-abling intellectual freedoms and confining social behaviors. And religion is defined as patriarchally for Moonshadow as it is for the characters in *The Chosen*. His father and the men of his company affect his spirituality far more than any of the women in his life do.

Religion dictates social behavior for many teenagers in fiction. Reuven and Danny in *The Chosen* attend the schools they do, eat the foods they do, and choose the careers they do because of their reactions to religious dictates placed on them by their fathers. In *Dragonwings*, Moonshadow believes his father's dreams of flying because of the filial piety expected of him by his religion. The boy sacrifices his own sense of community and his education to support his father's spirituality. And Opal Ringer in Kerr's *What I Really Think of You* is forbidden the peer-pressure-defined material comforts she desires. Moreover, she is pressured by her parents to adopt a gender role that upholds biblical teachings. Her parents expect her to be submissive and to follow scriptural dictates. Like Danny and Moonshadow, Opal renounces secular comforts and gender equality because her father's approval proves more impor-tant to her than rebellion.

*What I Really Think of You* alternates between two first-person narrators, Opal Ringer and Jesse Pegler. Both teenagers have fa-thers who are preachers, although like the two main characters in *The Chosen*, one character belongs to a more conservative sect of the same religion since Opal's father is more evangelical than the charismatic televangelist Guy Pegler. The tension between these teenagers and their fathers is exacerbated by the Oedipal struggle both of their elder brothers are staging with their fathers. Thus, not only does Opal have to negotiate the disparities between her sense of self and her father's sense of self, but she also has to watch her brother, Bobby John, negotiate a far more painful rift with their authoritarian father, while Jesse watches his brother, Bud, negotiate a similar rift. The four children of these two authoritarian men are understandably perplexed by the role of religion in their own thinking; they confuse religious authority with their fathers' authority. Opal's father reminds her brother that "a child should be beholden to his father" (3). Jesse cannot seem to love God because he cannot love his father. When Opal experiences a religious transformation that unifies her relationship with her father, Jesse feels more estranged from his religious heritage than ever. He identifies as his worst fear becoming the type of religious leader his father and brother are (150).

For Opal, the tension between the secular life and religious life is defined as a series of discursive dichotomies. She positions her narrative as a tale she is telling an unsympathetic audience: "You always used to laugh. I never had to do much more than just show up and you'd all start nudging each other with grins starting to tip your mouths" (1). She describes herself as a "have-not" in conflict with others who are "haves" (19) and often wonders such things as whether she would choose between eating off china plates with sterling cutlery or joining Christ in the Rapture (65). For her, the two things are incompatible. As a result, she experiences a Cartesian struggle between her thoughts and her flesh: "I got to wondering again what death was, anyway, and if there really was a Satan's hell, or was it all words and no one really knew anything, just made things up" (63). Her mother tells her that "rapture" and "ecstasy" are "Words, honey. Words can't always say what things mean," driving at the split between ideas and the physical world that so troubles Opal (122). She further identifies religion as more discursive than tangible when she tells her mother that the Rapture is not ever going to come: "We just always say it's coming when we can't take what's already here" (140). Just as televangelist Guy Pegler has learned that appearances matter more than sanctity in his televised business of saving souls, Opal feels disenchanted when she suspects religion is more a matter of rhetoric than of practice. And like Guy Pegler's sons, Opal suspects her parents use religious authority to assert their parental authority over her.

Two ironic actions further complicate the notion of religious authority in *What I Really Think of You*. Jesse Pegler's father rejects him because he is not pious enough to meet his father's standards. Offsetting Guy Pegler's hypocrisy is one of the only noble actions in the narrative: Jesse promises to care for a dying man's dog, thereby mitigating the old man's final concern. Guy Pegler profits from his son's action by broadcasting it on his show, and his church inherits all of the man's assets. Jesse, on the other hand, is happy simply to have alleviated someone else's emotional pain. As the book ends, he is still disaffected from his family and church, but he seems to accept himself. He has rebelled against his father's religious institution and found transcendent peace. Meanwhile, Opal has spoken in tongues, herself enacting a ritual for which she once derided her mother. The once-questioning Opal is the most ardent Christian in the narrative by its conclusion. She reveals that "what she really thinks" of the "haves" to whom the story is addressed is that she loves them, even though they have systematically excluded her from their ranks. Her religious fervor is perhaps sullied, however, by its exact coincidence with her falling in love with Jesse's older brother, Bud. The cynical reader might question the nature of the passion Opal feels. Kerr is certainly asserting an ideology that blind faith is, indeed, blind.

*The Chosen, Dragonwings,* and *What I Really Think of You* portray religion as an institution that is patriarchal and discursive. Competing discourses defined largely by their fathers lead the characters in these novels first to rebel and then to accept some variation of the status quo that is socially acceptable. For all of these characters, accepting or rejecting their father's heritage becomes central to their ability to exist within the status quo. They cannot find a place in the culture at large until they understand the discourses of their own religious culture.

## Identity Politics

"Identity politics" refers to the social affiliations that members of any society construct to position people in relationship to one another. Although certainly not constituted as monolithic institutions, identity politics nevertheless take on institutional dimensions in the ways that people who share affiliations conform to the expectations of their identified social position. Religion is one type of identity politics: Jews define many behaviors in terms of their religious behaviors, as do Christians, Muslims, or Buddhists. Social class constitutes another form of identity politics: people of various social classes often conform to the mores of their culture without even realizing they are doing so. Those who rebel against the mores of their social class are still identified in terms of the institution they are rejecting: their behavior as rebels is defined in terms of what they reject about social class as an institution.

Identity politics are a social construction. That is, they are defined by discourse, not biology. Social constructions play a determining role in how we perceive ourselves politically. Gender, it has been argued, is a political construct, constructed to repress women. As Barbara Johnson puts it: "the question of gender is a question of language" (37).[6] The same is certainly true of race: racial difference and racism are embedded in discourse. Indeed, Henry Louis Gates Jr. focuses on the trope of the signifying monkey precisely because that trickster figure is a discursively aware figure. Gates asserts that a meta-awareness of discursiveness informs all African-American literature (xx–xxi). Moreover, he provides Ralph Ellison's discursively self-conscious definition of blackness to support the contention that race is situated in discourse:

> It is not skin color which makes a Negro American but cultural heritage as shaped by the American experiences, the social and political predicament; a sharing of that "concord of sensibilities" which the group expressed through historical circumstance and through which it has come to constitute a subdivision of the larger American culture. (quoted 121)

Not biological factors but cultural heritage, which is determined by language, creates racial difference in America. Cornel West insists that racism can be analyzed only if we consider it in terms of discursive conditions that allow for racism, in terms of the institutions that perpetuate it, and in terms of the experiences of domination and resistance in the lives of African Americans (268). Race, like gender, is an institution that is inseparable from discourse and power.

Just as race and gender are issues in Virginia Hamilton's dystopia *The Gathering* and Laurence Yep's *Dragonwings*, race, gender, and class create another type of defining institution in adolescent literature: identity politics. These concepts serve as institutions because the behaviors of large numbers of people are regulated in terms of identity politics. And whether people self-select the characteristics associated with a group or whether those characteristics are imposed on them by the perception of others, their sense of affiliation with a group serves in some way as a limiting factor. Take the example provided by the stereotypes in the title of John Gray's book alone: *Men Are from Mars, Women Are from Venus.* Some people accept such stereotypes, others reject them, but all members of the gendered group "men" are subjected to certain sets of societal expectations typified by these stereotypes, as are members of the group women. Even the rebellions of those who reject gender roles are at least partially determined by a societally shared concept of the institutions of femininity and masculinity.

Gender and race constitute identity politics that are, as Robyn Wiegman notes, too often determined by an "epistemology of the visual" (8): we define race and gender in terms of physical appearance. Although a character like the androgynous protagonist of Peter Pohl's *Johnny, My Friend* (1985) confounds the epistemology of the visual by cross-dressing and although a character like the protagonist of Nella Larsen's *Passing* (1929) demonstrates that it is possible for some people to use temporarily the epistemology of the visual to their advantage, Wiegman's analysis of gender and race is one of many that problematizes how relying on looks to define identity leads to essentialism — that is, defining people's "essential" inner traits as biologically determined.[7]

Identity politics matter most in adolescent literature, however, in terms of how an adolescent's self-identifications position her within her culture. How an adolescent defines herself in terms of race, gender, and class often determines her access to power in her specific situation. We can surface the myriad intricacies that affect identity politics in a YA novel if we ask ourselves, "Who controls the discourse in this narrative?" Mae Gwendolyn Henderson suggests analyzing the "dialogic of differences" and the "dialectic of identity" to get at the power struggles embedded in a narrative. She defines the "dialogic of differences" as the discourses that occur between the Self and Other and the "dialectic of identity" as the dialogue with Self that occurs internally (19). She further complicates the tension at work in a text by breaking her analysis into "competing and complementary" discourses, so that the critic is confronted with at least four levels of discursive analysis: those moments when the individual competes with the Other, those when s/he agrees with the Other, those when s/he affirms herself, and those when s/he experiences internal discord (23). Analyzing these discursive levels in Mildred Taylor's *The Road to Memphis* (1990) demonstrates how one character, Cassie Logan, defines herself in terms of the institutions of race, class, and gender.

When Cassie describes the black community in which she lives in southern Mississippi, she employs a discourse of consensus. She notes the ways that the black families help each other, and the picture she portrays of this community is one of relative harmony. Cassie and her brothers are even able to maintain a long-term friendship with a white boy, Jeremy Simms, who claims, "folks is just folks" when asked why he refuses to participate in the racism that surrounds him (41). His comment marks the ability for an interaction between individual and Other that is marked by consensus, not conflict. But when Cassie describes the interaction between the rest of the white community and the black community in Strawberry, Mississippi, she demonstrates discursive conflict with the Other. Local boys terrify her friend Harris, first taunting him, then forcing him to run as the "coon" in their "coon hunt." The horrible wordplay that the boys are enacting shows the power of language to harm: Harris never recovers either emotionally or physically from having physically enacted the racial epitaph "coon."

Another of Cassie's friends, Moe, also shows the relationship between discourse and action. Although he suffers through the indignity of this same group of white boys rubbing his head for luck, when they begin making lewd comments about Cassie the discourse of conflict overwhelms him, and he strikes all three of them with a tire iron. Cassie and her brother Stacey help Moe escape to Memphis with the help of their white friend Jeremy. And on the road, they experience another discursive situation fraught with conflict when a white gas station attendant refuses Cassie access to the rest room. Because of the physical urgency she is feeling, Cassie stands outside the open rest room door, tempted to go in despite the posted sign that reads "WHITE LA-DIES ONLY" (177). Cassie experiences an internal conflict with her own identity as she contemplates this situation: "I knew perfectly well the kind of trouble I'd be in if I disobeyed the signs. I knew perfectly well that I would be breaking the law if I did. Still, as I stood there facing those signs I felt such an anger, such a hostility, such a need to defy them that I couldn't walk right on past" (177). Cassie attempts to violate the institutional structures that prohibit her from urinating because of this internal conflict. She is willing to ignore the words on the door, even though she knows they are signifiers of the discursively constituted law upheld by the government in Mississippi, to preserve her own sense of self. She places her hand on the rest room door, pushes it open, and is immediately prevented from relieving herself by a white woman who verbally accosts her. Although Cassie has not technically broken the law since she has neither entered the facility nor used it, the discursive conflict that erupts at the gas station becomes physically violent. Trying to run away from the attendant, who also verbally abuses her, Cassie slips and falls. He kicks her "like somebody with no heart would kick a dog" (179). She feels so humiliated she is stunned beyond language. In Cassie's interaction with the white Other, she feels temporarily transformed into an animal. Her conflict with the Other is so great that she no longer shares a language with him. This passage depicts powerfully the horror of power differentials that go unchecked: the gas station attendant physically assaults Cassie because he knows he is privileged by the discourse of his culture that allows white people power over black people, males power over females, and adults power over teenagers. Knowing that nothing in the institutions within which she must exist can protect her, Cassie falls silent, as Jeremy Simms falls silent when his friends accuse him of racism (77), as Cassie and her friends fall silent when confronted with their white peers' racism (68, 117–118, 122). When racism is stronger as an institution than any discursive power these adolescents have, they retreat from discourse with the Other as fully as they can. They rely instead on an internal dialogue, an identity discourse of consensus, that allows them to self-affirm even though the Other refuses to legitimize them.

Gender is also reinforced as an institution in this culture, as it is in all cultures, by discourse. Cassie experiences the discourse as conflict with the Other when her grandmother nags her to be more feminine, when white boys treat her as a sex object, and when her own brother silences her (48, 68, 90–91, 95).[8] She denigrates marriage as an institution that would hinder her education: "Body had to take care of some man and a whole bunch of children, she wouldn't ever have time for school" (146). She recognizes the power differential between men and women in her culture. Because she does not like it, she knows to limit the number of men who will have power over her by remaining celibate. Her girlfriend Sissy provides a foil relationship when she gets pregnant by a boy who ultimately dies. By the end of the novel, the once eloquent Sissy seems to be one of the least powerful characters in the novel. Her final utterance is a scream when she acknowledges her fiancé's death: like those confronted with racism, she retreats from language when the discourse reinforcing her powerlessness becomes too overwhelming (280).

Offsetting Cassie's discourse of conflict with the Other about gender is her discourse of consensus with herself. She is a character who enjoys her own femininity, thinking as she looks in a mirror, "I was pretty and I knew it. I didn't think much about it, though. It was just one of those things I was, and I didn't dwell on it, except for when I had on something especially nice and was wanting to look my best" (58). Later, she thinks, "I was quite pleased with how I looked" (82). She even allows herself to enjoy feeling sexual attraction to a lawyer she meets on the way to Memphis, Solomon Bradley. When he kisses her, she thinks, "those few seconds had been enough to make me feel what I had never felt. My legs were weak. My body was trembling. My thoughts were racing. My head was in a cloud and all my thinking was blurred" (252). Cassie enjoys looking good because she enjoys the sexual power she has over men, but she also discovers that she enjoys experiencing a sense of being overpowered by a man's sexuality. That her thoughts are both racing and blurred indicates the dynamic of her internal discourse about gender: she is at once thinking many things and thinking indistinct things. She is enjoying her own power and someone else's. Cassie may rebel against the way women are treated in her culture, just as she rebels against the way whites treat blacks, but that does not mean she wants to become what is to her the Other: she feels self-acceptance of herself as black and female. That Cassie is able to maintain an affirmative discourse of identity with herself about sex and race demonstrates that adolescents can be empowered within — and despite —identity politics as institutions.

Knowledge of racism and sexism allows Cassie some degree of power — when she recognizes totalizing discourses, she can reject them. Her inability to recognize the class discourse that surrounds her, however, makes her more subject to its oppression. As Jameson notes, awareness of class-consciousness is a precursor to resisting oppression (*Political Unconscious* 289). Many of the individuals who experience racist discourse in this novel as conflict between the Self and Other are simultaneously experiencing the oppression of class privilege. Their seeming lack of awareness about the power that economics plays in this situation exacerbates the discourse of conflict. None of the characters acknowledges anything more about the unfairness of social class than their desire to own land because they recognize that tenant farming makes it impossible for sharecroppers (black or white) to make a profit. Taylor, however, is careful to embed class tensions into the narrative. The white boys who taunt Harris, Cassie, and Moe carry the markers of poor whites in the way that their clothing, their language, and their actions are depicted. These boys clearly perceive themselves as superior in social class to middle-class blacks like the Logan family. Yet Taylor does not attribute racism only to whites of a certain class: the sheriff of Strawberry, clearly educated and clearly possessing more material wealth than Jeremy Simms's family, refuses to believe that Jeremy would willingly help Moe escape punishment for assaulting three white boys with a tire iron: "We gotta believe that, all of us. We know that he wouldn't be turning his back on his own. We know that" (275). Moreover, the two white males in the text who refuse to participate in the discourse of racism come from vastly different classes: Jeremy Simms is poor and Mr. Jamison, the lawyer who gives Moe advice, is upper–middle class. Thus, although the narrative situation provides the reader with knowledge that social class contributes to oppression, the characters seem unaware that racism feeds the class dialectic. Their lack of knowledge contributes to their lack of social power, for when they fight racism or sexism, they are more empowered than when they do not.

Terry Eagleton maintains that the task of the trained reader is to read such "absences" as Cassie's failure to recognize the power embedded in social class in order to make "manifest those conditions of its making (inscribed in its very letter) about which it is necessarily silent" (43). Foucault focuses on the process of rereading, of returning to "those things registered in the interstices of the text, its gaps and absences" ("What" 135). To Jameson, class-conscious reading is imperative, given that art cannot be removed from its "cognitive and pedagogical dimensions" (*Political Unconscious* 50). Readers trained to pay attention to tensions that arise from such narrative silences can experience both a richer reading of the narrative and a better understanding of the role of discourse in regulating the relationship between power and knowledge in their own cultures. Ideally, teenage readers will also feel less repressed by the authoritarian social forces they perceive operating on them.

The YA novel, a genre that has emerged as an aspect of postmodernism, situates the individual as both comprised by institutional forces and compromised by them. Adolescents have power that becomes institutional power as they (necessarily) engage in the social forces that simultaneously empower and repress them. Multiple institutions affect the teenager: government agencies that regulate foster care and juvenile justice, Hollywood and Madison Avenue, the music industry, institutions such as Scouts and 4-H, which were initiated for the specific purpose of channeling teenagers' power. All YA novels depict some postmodern tension between individuals and institutions. And the tension is often depicted as residing within discursive constructs. Once protagonists of the YA novel have learned to discursively negotiate their place in the domination-repression chain of power, they are usually depicted as having grown, satisfying the conventions of the *Entwicklungsroman*.

I have tried in this chapter to demonstrate some principles that affect the dynamics of power and repression that individuals experience as institutions construct them. Numerous discursive issues surround these dynamics, so readers aware of ideologies, of the carnivalesque, of heteroglossia, and of the need to identify textual absences should have a variety of approaches with which to analyze adolescent characters' relationships to the institutions in their lives. Whether the institution under investigation is government, school, religion, identity politics, or another institution altogether matters less than the acknowledgment that institutions rely on language to regulate the individual's authority throughout the genre of the Young Adult novel.

### CHAPTER 3

# "Maybe that is writing, changing things around and disguising the for-real"

## THE PARADOX OF AUTHORITY IN

## ADOLESCENT LITERATURE

We can investigate power and repression in adolescent literature by analyzing textual discourses about institutional politics and social construction. We can also assess how adolescent literature is itself an institutional discourse that participates in the power and repression dynamic that socializes adolescents into their cultural positions: characters created by adult writers test the limits of their power within the context of multiple institutions for the benefit of adolescent readers who supposedly gain some benefit from experiencing this dynamic vicariously. Central to the construction of adolescent literature as a tool of socialization is the issue of how adult writers depict authority in the literature. The ways authority can be represented in adolescent literature are far too various for any one analysis of the genre to cover, but two manifestations of authority are representative of the ways literary texts model adolescents internalizing their place within a culture's power structure. The first of these, the relationship between parents and adolescents, testifies to the significance of adolescents' construction of the power/repression dynamic: adolescent characters themselves often create repressive parental figures to dominate them. The adolescents, in turn, rebel against this perceived domination in order to engage their own power. This phenomenon is observable in Jean Webster's *Daddy-Long-Legs* (1912) and Hamilton's *Planet of Junior Brown* (1971). The power struggles they create and resolve are internal to the text. The conflict with parent-as-authority-figure seems to be one of the most pervasive patterns in adolescent literature. Unsurprisingly, these rebellions against repression frequently prove to be redemptive for adolescents.

But since we know that it is not actual adolescents but adult authors who are constructing the repressive relationships that ultimately prove liberating to adolescent characters, we also need to investigate a second level of textual authority, that which resides within the narrative structure itself for the purpose of affecting the reader's subjectivity. Writers are another source of authority within adolescent literature as an institution. Investigating the ways that they employ aspects of narrative structure to manipulate the reader reveals much about the adolescent reader's potential empowerment and repression. Such novels as Hamilton's *Arilla Sun Down* (1976) and Chris Crutcher's *Staying Fat for Sarah Byrnes* (1993) demonstrate how issues of authority are embedded in the narrative structure of YA novels.

The study of textual narrative authority shows how pervasive authority and control are in teaching adolescent readers to accept power/repression relationships as inevitable, for the very construction of an ideologically positioned implied reader often displaces adolescent readers' potential for empowerment. In other words, studying parent figures in YA novels shows how often adolescent characters embrace repression as a precursor to empowerment, whereas studying narrative structure demonstrates that YA novels teach adolescent readers to accept a certain amount of repression as a cultural imperative. Thus, both characterization and narrative structure are wedded to adolescent literature's function of communicating to adolescents about cultural power and repression.

## Parents and Textual Authority

The role of parents in adolescent literature is one of the defining characteristics of the genre. Since Anglophone cultures, by and large, usually accept as a given the premise that adolescents must separate from their parents in order to grow, the literatures of these cultures reflect the same bias.[1] Thus, although children's novels often have absent parents so that the child protagonist is free to have an adventure (as in *Alice in Wonderland*, *The Children of Green Knowe*, *Zeely*, or *From the Mixed-Up Files of Mrs. Basil E. Frankweiler*), the child often returns to some sort of parent-based home by the end of the narrative. Perry Nodelman implies that the core value of children's literature is "security," so when children return to home and family at the end of a children's book, they are doing so to achieve a sense of security (*Pleasures* 78–79). Parents of teenagers constitute a more problematic presence in the adolescent novel because parent-figures in YA novels usually serve more as sources of conflict than as sources of support. They are more likely to repress than to empower. Danny's rejection of his father's religion in *The Chosen*, for example, is in part a Freudian attempt to castrate his father, but the boy's desire to disempower the man is a direct result of Danny's experience of being patriarchally repressed. Even if parent figures are absent from an adolescent novel, their physical absence often creates a psychological presence that is remarked upon as a sort of repression felt strongly by the adolescent character. This absence then becomes, in turn, a presence against which the adolescent character rebels. When adolescent characters transform an absent character into a presence against which they can rebel, they are creating a parent who is present as *logos*, as Word, through which and against which to develop.

That the adolescent would rely on the Symbolic Order to create a parent figure is a central tenet of Freudian and Lacanian analysis. Roderick McGillis provides an accessible overview of many concepts important to Lacanian analysis as they apply to adolescent literature. I quote here at length because of the elegance with which McGillis defines a complex topic:

> Lacan articulates the notion of the "Other" most famously in his essay on the "mirror-stage" of development (see *Écrits* 1–7). This stage occurs when the infant — sometime between the ages of six and eighteen months — becomes aware of herself or himself when faced with his or her image in a mirror. What the infant sees is an illusion, a reversed image of the self that appears to be someone else and yet is discernibly the self. The moment for Lacan is crucial, for it initiates what he refers to as the "Imaginary": that is, a relationship with the world based on the image, on what one sees and how one is seen. The Imaginary is pre-verbal, yet it also continues to exist once the child enters what Lacan calls the "Symbolic," the world of language and the laws that language brings. Essentially, the mirror stage inaugurates what Lacan terms a misrecognition (*méconnaissance*)

because the subject observes what appears to be an "Ideal-I," a person whole and entire, capable and independent. The attachment to this "Ideal-I" is ambiguous because the "Ideal-I" remains something both devoutly to be desired and irritatingly out of reach. (McGillis, "Another Kick" 42)

The child enters the Symbolic Order upon learning language. Lacan demonstrates that at this stage, it is not so much the actual father that a child rebels against, it is the symbolic father who interferes with the child's desire for his mother that creates the conflict within the child's mind. Lacan describes the Symbolic Order into which a child enters when he begins this conflict as the "Name-of-the-Father" (*Écrits* 199); the child is thus in conflict with the Symbolic Order, that is, the phallic signifier, language.[2] The crucial action for the child, then, is to somehow eliminate the threat of the symbolic father, "thus showing that if this murder is the fruitful moment of debt through which the subject binds himself for life to the Law, the symbolic Father is, in so far as he signifies this Law, the dead Father" (*Écrits* 199). Without going into the nuances of psychosis that Lacan explores or the nuances of gender that he fails to explore, I would like to point out that this principle demonstrates a major convention at work in novels about adolescence: regardless of whether the adolescent has an actual parent figure to rebel against (or, in more Oedipal terms, to symbolically murder), the child must create for her- or himself a parent figure, a symbolic parent, to murder.[3]

Three different situations lead to three different sets of Oedipal struggle (as I loosely call the struggle of the adolescent against the parent that seems to be a rebellion permeating the genre of the adolescent novel). The first of these is the involvement of the actual parent in the adolescent's development, as in *Little Women* (1868, 1869), *Seventeenth Summer*, or *M. C. Higgins, the Great* (1974). The second is the involvement of a parent figure *in loco parentis*, as in *Adventures of Huckleberry Finn* (1885) or *The Outsiders*. The non-involvement of an actual parent can create a third type of adolescent fiction wherein the adolescent creates a parent of words, *in logos parentis*, as in Jean Webster's *Daddy-Long-Legs* and Virginia Hamilton's *The Planet of Junior Brown*. I recognize that this phrase I have coined, "*in logos parentis*," is a violent yoking together of heterogeneous languages, but it is nonetheless useful to the point I wish to make.

## In Parentis

One of the most frequently commented on features of the prototype of female adolescent literature, Louisa May Alcott's *Little Women,* is the novel's involved parents, especially Marmee.[4] Marmee works diligently to help her daughters become socially indoctrinated "little women." She tells the two eldest, Meg and Jo: "I want my daughters to be beautiful, accomplished, and good; to be admired, loved and respected; to have a happy youth, to be well and wisely married, and to lead useful, pleasant lives, with as little care and sorrow to try them as God sees fit to send. To be loved and chosen by a good man is the best and sweetest thing which can happen to a woman; and I sincerely hope my girls may know this beautiful experience" (89). Toward that end, Marmee is closely involved in her daughters' growth. She gains a particularly strong authoritative presence in Jo's life when she tries to help Jo obliterate her expressions of anger. Jo's father, too, is critical of and involved in Jo's suppression of her temper. Jo gives her parents the most authority she grants them in the entire text when she agrees with their combined agenda to repress her temper. Jo's subsequent rebellion against her parents is very short-lived: she writes lurid potboilers only until she is corrected by the well-meaning Professor Bhaer, acting *in loco parentis,* whom she eventually marries. Jo ultimately grows up to be exactly what her parents have wanted her to be all along: a self-eviscerated matron serving the patriarchy.[5] Although Jo may act out the father-daughter fantasy that Madelon Bedell cites as the defining pattern of the Alcott canon, Jo never does quite manage to rebel against her mother (241–242). As Elizabeth Keyser notes, "Marmee keeps her daughters dependent, undeveloped, diminutive" by teaching them to repress their own desires (69). Marmee, and to a lesser degree, Mr. March, serves as the source of narrative authority designed to repress an adolescent's power.

If *Little Women* is a prototypical nineteenth-century novel of female adolescence, Maureen Daly's *Seventeenth Summer* could be called the twentieth-century prototype.[6] As with Jo, Angie's mother is more present in her life than her father is, for as a traveling salesman, he is gone during the week. As with Jo, Angie's rebellion against her bourgeois parents (in this case, staged when she dates a boy from the working-class — gasp!) is short-lived. Angie ends up doing exactly what her parents wanted her to do all along: she breaks up with Jack and goes to college. Angie's parents barely figure in the plot of the novel; they are present in relatively few scenes. But as Angie internalizes their values and acts on their wishes, she demonstrates a self-repression of which they clearly approve. Based on *Seventeenth Summer* and *Little Women*, it would seem, then, that in classic novels of adolescent female development, the Oedipal stage is short-lived for the female protagonist.[7]

The pattern for males is a bit different, for their rebellions seem to gain them some degree of autonomy that females whose parents are present in their lives have traditionally been denied.[8] Virginia Hamilton's *M. C. Higgins, the Great* is the story of a boy's efforts to reform his stubborn father. M. C. recognizes that the waste from the strip-mining above their family's land on Sara's Mountain is about to destroy their home. The boy tries to convince his father, Jones, to move away from the land, but he is unsuccessful. The tension with his father is demonstrated by their swimming competition; when M. C. can finally swim the Ohio River, Jones rewards his son with a phallic forty-foot flagpole on which M. C. perches. The tension between them becomes palpable when M. C. befriends a boy that his father has prohibited him from seeing because of intraracial racism. Based on what he learns from this forbidden family, M. C. comes to realize that his father will never leave the land, so the boy decides to build a wall to protect his family from the strip-mining waste. And his rebellion pays off, for his father helps build the wall, contributing gravestones from the family graveyard that are symbolic of the family's heritage. Through his rebellion, M. C. has gained his father's respect. M. C. learns to share some measure of authority with his father. Male protagonists experience a similar pattern of conflict transformed into cooperation in Laurence Yep's *Dragonwings*, Chris Crutcher's *Running Loose* (1983), and Jacqueline Woodson's *From the Notebooks of Melanin Sun* (1995).[9] Adolescent characters whose power is sanctioned by their parents are usually male, and they are far more likely to share authority with their parents than they are to usurp it altogether.

## In Loco Parentis

The substitute parent as a presence against which the adolescent can react is at least as old a convention as Clemens's *Adventures of Huckleberry Finn*. It is a critical commonplace to say that Jim is a surrogate father who replaces the inadequate Pap and gives Huck the parenting he has always needed; Aidan Chambers actually identifies Jim as being "*in loco parentis* to Huck" ("All of a Tremble" 203). In fact, in identifying the homoerotic archetype at work in *Adventures of Huckleberry Finn*, Leslie Fiedler casts Jim in the role of father figure in Huck's Oedipal crisis. But as with an actual parent, Huck must rebel against this *in loco parentis* figure before he can grow. Huck treats Jim with disrespect, fooling him about the fog on the river, until Jim teaches him that treating a loved one that way is "trash" (90). Huck must wrestle with his conscience about whether to sell out his father figure in a classically Oedipal maneuver: what better way to rid oneself of an authority figure than to sell him back into slavery? Luckily for Jim — and for Huck's sense of self — Huck ultimately changes his intentions, but the ultimate authority of the text still resides with Jim. It is he who carries the epistemological truth that enables the text's resolution: Huck's father figure tells him that his actual father is dead.

Ponyboy Curtis's rebellion against an *in loco parentis* figure in S. E. Hinton's *The Outsiders* is even more clear-cut. Ponyboy's brother, Daryl, has been his legal guardian since the death of their parents. Out of fear and insecurity, Daryl is verbally abusive to his brother because he knows no other way to control him. Ponyboy, interpreting this abusiveness as a lack of love, rebels against his brother's overstated authority. Pony cannot grow to maturity until he can understand his brother's strictness as an act of love; in other words, he cannot mature until he accepts and forgives his symbolic father figure. From this point in the novel, the two are capable of sharing authority. In Ursula K. LeGuin's *A Wizard of*

*Earthsea* (1968), Ged rebels against the wizard who has trained him before he learns how to use power appropriately. Dicey Tillerman has a similar experience with her grandmother in Cynthia Voigt's *The Homecoming* (1981) and *Dicey's Song* (1982): she rebels against Gram before the two decide to share the authority of raising the younger Tillerman children together. Thus, even if the parental figures are surrogates rather than actual, it seems that adolescents must rebel against them in order to grow.

## In Logos Parentis

What really strikes me as odd, however, is the propensity of adolescents with neither actual nor effective surrogate parents to create imaginary parents against whom to rebel in a classic re-enactment of the Lacanian principle of creating the Name-of-the-Father. After all, it would seem that the parentless adolescent is the most free, that being parentless is the most desirable imaginable state of adolescent wish fulfillment. Why would the adolescent create a parent to make trouble for him- or herself? Lacan might answer that the adolescent does so because the idea of the parent is so seductive, so central to the subject's sense of self-definition, that the process becomes inevitable:

> How can the Name-of-the-Father be called by the subject to the only place in which it could have reached him and in which it has never been? Simply by a real father, not necessarily by the subject's own father, but by A-father.
>
> Again, this A-father must attain that place to which the subject was unable to call him before. It is enough that this A-father should be situated in a third position in some relation based on the imaginary dyad, . . . ego-object or reality-ideal, that interests the subject in the field of eroticized aggression that it induces. (*Écrits* 217)

The most classic example of an adolescent who invents a parent out of words, an "A-father," to rebel against in what becomes an act of eroticized aggression is Judy Abbott, the protagonist of Jean Webster's epistolary *Bildungsroman, Daddy-Long-Legs.* The politics of authority are intricate and insidious in *Daddy-Long-Legs.*

Rescued from an orphanage by one of the institution's trustees who prefers to remain nameless, Judy attends college funded by her patron's beneficence. One condition her benefactor stipulates is that she write him a letter once a month: "Just such a letter as you would write to your parents if they were living" (16); the second condition crucial to Judy's rebellion is the benefactor's refusal to name himself. Because Judy does not know her benefactor or understand his motives, she attributes almost godlike authority to this anonymous man.

Although Judy's letters are supposed to be written to "Mr. John Smith," her first attempt to reject her benefactor's authority is to refuse this epithet: "Why couldn't you have picked out a name with a little personality? I might as well write letters to Dear Hitching-Post or Dear Clothes-Pole" (21). Both of the suggested names she dismisses are phallic. Because she has seen his shadow on the wall as he left the orphanage, she knows he is tall. She decides to address him as "Daddy-Long-Legs," another phallic name which comfortably evokes for her the parentage she seeks and which sets up an Oedipal tension for the reader to observe. Judy tells Daddy-Long-Legs: "I have been thinking about you a great deal this summer; having somebody take an interest in me after all these years, makes me feel as though I had found a sort of family. It seems as though I belonged to somebody now, and it's a very comfortable sensation" (21).

Judy then goes on to make up attributes she ascribes to Daddy-Long-Legs. For example, she decides what he looks like:

> I have it planned exactly what you look like — very satisfactorily — until I reach the top of your head, and then I *am* stuck. I can't decide whether you have white hair or black hair or sort of sprinkly gray hair or maybe none at all. . . . Would you like to know what color your eyes are? They're gray and your eyebrows stick out like a porch roof . . . and your mouth is a straight line with a tendency to turn down at the corners. Oh, you see, I know! You're a snappy old thing with a temper. (35)

In point of fact, Daddy-Long-Legs is nowhere near as old as she thinks; he is Jarvis Pendleton, the forty-year-old uncle of one of her roommates, who is "tall and thinnish with a dark face all over lines, and the funniest underneath smile that never quite comes through but just wrinkles up the corners of his mouth. And he has a way of making you feel right off as though you'd known him a long time. He's very companionable" (59). Judy does not discover the identity of Daddy-Long-Legs or his sexual interest in her until the final scene of the novel. That Jarvis has knowledge Judy does not gives him power over her in a situation in which shared authority is impossible.

Over and over, Judy rebels against the lack of knowledge she has about her benefactor. Lying beneath her peevishness is a feeling of the disproportionate power in her situation; she seeks information about him to equalize the imbalance that comes from his knowing everything about her and her knowing nothing about him. The power imbalance exists entirely within the Symbolic Order, for Judy knows that although she is actual to him, he can never be more than symbolic for her.[10] She writes:

> Sir: You never answer any questions; you never show the slightest interest in anything I do. You are probably the horridest one of all those horrid trustees, and the reason you are educating me is, not because you care a bit about me, but from a sense of duty. I don't know a single thing about you. I don't even know your name. It is very uninspiring writing to a thing. I haven't a doubt but that you throw my letters into the wastebasket without reading them. (47)

Daddy-Long-Legs does, however, read her letters, as he makes clear after she writes that she plans to spend the summer with her roommate, Sallie McBride, and her family. Judy has made no bones about enjoying the attention Sallie's brother Jimmie has paid her, so she is hurt and angry when her benefactor's secretary writes forbidding her to go to the McBrides'. Judy cannot know what the reader eventually ascertains — that Pendleton must be jealous of McBride — so she rebels by refusing to write to him for a while in the summer. Since he exists as a symbolic figure only when she writes to him and since she is rebelling against his efforts to sublimate her sexuality, he is effectively dead for the duration of her silence, temporarily killed by her aggression. When she resumes her correspondence and resuscitates this symbolic father, she tells him, "It has been nearly two months since I wrote, which wasn't nice of me, I know, but I haven't loved you much this summer — you see I'm being frank" (108). If readers have discerned that Daddy-Long-Legs is Jarvis Pendleton, they may recognize that some of Judy's frustration is sexualized; readers with that perception understand that the figure Judy thinks she loves filially is entirely fabricated. As such, Daddy-Long-Legs is a construct of the Symbolic Order.

Judy rebels against Daddy-Long-Legs again the following summer when he offers to send her to Europe. She insists, instead, that she should work tutoring to earn money for herself. Jarvis Pendleton — for whom she is developing feelings perhaps more legitimate than the gratitude-blown-into-love she feels for Daddy-Long-Legs — has also pressured her to go to Europe. Judy writes to her benefactor in language with a subtly sexual undertone: if Jarvis "hadn't been so dictatorial, maybe I should have entirely weakened. I can be enticed step by step, but I *won't* be forced" (150). Judy's sense of rebelliousness is well developed; thus, it is no surprise that later in the summer she joins the McBrides at their summer camp without consulting Daddy-Long-Legs. Although Pendleton is performing *in loco parentis* and Judy rebels against it, her more significant rebellion is against the parent she has created symbolically, *in logos parentis*.

The novel takes its most ironic turn in the final pages when Judy discovers that Jarvis Pendleton has been her benefactor all along. The passage is ironic — unintentionally so, which thus leaves the novel an easy mark for deconstruction — because for once Judy, who has been so independent, so assertive, and so rebellious throughout the entire novel, does not utter a single word of protest that Pendleton has deceived her, possibly even manipulating her Pygmalion-style to create the perfect little wife for himself. Instead, she meekly puts her hand in his as he "laughed and held out [his] hand and said, 'Dear little Judy, couldn't you guess that I was Daddy-Long-Legs?'" (186).

As it turns out, Judy *has* had a surrogate parent *in loco parentis* against whom to rebel throughout the course of the novel, but because she has not known that, because her understanding of her parent figure has been something she has constructed out of the Symbolic Order to meet her own needs, the novel fits the paradigm of the *in logos parentis* narrative: Daddy-Long-Legs is a parent in name and word only. And Judy successfully completes the

growth to adulthood that the *bildungsroman* pattern demands because she has had this parent figure made of words against whom
to rebel. She has empowered herself by rebelling against a parental
authority figure.

In *The Planet of Junior Brown* by Virginia Hamilton, Junior Brown
has much the same experience of creating a parent out of words.
Unlike Judy, he does have one actual parent present in his life, the
overbearing and neurotic Junella Brown. Her presence as the repressive parent in Junior's story underscores the triadic pattern
Lacan considers central to the Oedipal struggle: the son's struggle
grows out of "dependence on [his mother's] love . . . the desire
for her desire" situated against the "phallocentric" parent blocking
this desire (*Écrits* 198). Junior Brown would like to make his
mother happy, but Mrs. Brown is so authoritative that she has
effectively silenced her son: although he is a virtuoso pianist, she
has removed the strings from his piano. She has "tak[en] away his
sound from him" so that "she has her peace and quiet" (118–119).
And just as Mrs. Brown has silenced Junior's aural art, she silences
(or darkens) his visual art by taking his paints away from him and
destroying his masterpiece when she does not like what he has
painted. Junior's pre-Oedipal desire for imaginary oneness with
his mother is clearly impossible.[11]

Junior, who weighs over three hundred pounds, misses his father. The man's absence rather than his presence seems to be the
chief obstacle in Junior's relationship with his mother because
Mrs. Brown seems incapable of happiness with her husband gone.
As a result of Junior's misguided goals for happiness, he seems to
have no existence of his own; his very name makes him a lesser
parallel to, a shadow of, his absent father. Whether to counter-
balance his unexpressed rage at his mother or simply out of long-
ing, Junior describes the existence of a father in a way that makes
the man seem tangible. But a close reading of the text reveals the
possibility that Mr. Brown is, like Daddy-Long-Legs, *in logos parentis*, a parent constructed of words by an adolescent who needs to
believe in this invented figure.

Early in the narrative, Junior's friend Buddy thinks about information Junior has given him: "Junior Brown's mother was as
out of her head anxious as all the other women in the neighbor-
hood whose husbands had gone away. Only, Junior's father had a

good job over in Jersey" (25). The euphemism for the men who have abandoned their families coupled with the euphemism for Mrs. Brown's neuroses establishes the possibility that the text is not being entirely honest here. Since the information comes to the reader through Junior's best friend's impression of Junior's interpretation, the possibility of distorted facts seems even more likely.

More possibilities of textual misleading arise later in the narrative: "On Saturday morning Walter Brown didn't stand there at the threshold of Junior's room. Half asleep, Junior knew his father wasn't there. 'Daddy,' he said because he wanted to" (104). Even before he is conscious, Junior is aware of his father's absence. Then Junior demonstrates his ability to fabricate his father's presence with his apostrophic evocation of his father's name. The text continues: "His father might have come in the room wearing his robe and slippers and freshly creased slacks. He always did come in to Junior in a warm, respectful manner, as if Junior's room were the chapel he had known all his life" (104). In Junior's mind, his father is dressed like a priest and his room is the temple; the boy himself becomes the god about to be worshiped by the robed man. Junior needs this vision of his father to offset the denigration he suffers at his mother's hands. And then Junior says out loud in a "voice . . . husky with feeling": "Daddy . . . I haven't seen you on a Saturday morning in forever" (104). The statement could be literally true; perhaps Junior has never met his father. Junior's knowledge about his father is a power the boy does not want. He exists in denial rather than proclaim his father absent.

Junior's friend Buddy Clark provides a foil for his father-lessness; Buddy, too, is fatherless (and also motherless) in a much more visible way than Junior is. Buddy is a homeless child who scarcely remembers his parents. He has learned to be self-sufficient and how to help other children in similar circumstances. Buddy has two adult mentors: the newspaper vendor for whom he works and the janitor at the school who helps both Buddy and Junior hide in the school basement so that they will not have to face the madding crowd at their public school. As Junior is an artistic genius, Buddy is a mathematical genius, so neither of them conforms to the community in which they are forced to exist. The janitor, Mr. Pool, helps them construct a solar system in the basement, and Buddy surprises Junior by building a tenth planet for the system and naming it "the planet of Junior Brown." But Junior, unsure how to accept love from these friends, thinks they are making fun of him.

Buddy is able to grow during the course of the novel because of the help of the two men who function for him *in loco parentis*. Of Mr. Pool, Buddy thinks, "If he could have a father, he would have only this man" (166). Yet Buddy temporarily rebels against Pool when the janitor interferes with the boy's plan for helping Junior run away. Junior has been driven to the brink of insanity by his mother's repression. After his mother has destroyed Junior's painting, he decides to run away, rejecting her and rebelling against his hope of his father's return. The fantasy that his father will come rescue him on Saturday no longer seems enough to sustain the boy; this breakdown of the Symbolic Order appears to be leading Junior into the type of psychosis that Lacan describes (*Écrits* 192–201). Junior's emotional vulnerability is further exacerbated by the schizophrenia of his piano teacher, Miss Peebs. Trying to help his teacher, Junior tells Miss Peebs he will take "the relative" who has been plaguing her away. But "the relative" is a figment of Miss Peebs's paranoid imagination. In order to rid her of it, Junior takes "the relative" on as his own personal paranoid delusion. He has again constructed another male relative in his own mind to authorize a mother figure's happiness.

Mr. Pool thinks that Buddy should turn Junior over to the authorities, but Buddy thinks that to do so would make Junior crazier, so Buddy decides instead to take his friend to the "planet" in the basement of an abandoned building where he and other homeless boys have built a hideout. After rebelling against his father *in loco parentis*, Buddy has the greatest moment of growth of any character in the novel. He remembers that the boy who taught him how to survive on the streets taught him not that "the highest law is to learn to live for yourself" as he has inaccurately remembered (74), but that "We are together . . . because we have to learn to live for each other" (217). Once Buddy understands the fundamental importance of community in his life, his whole life changes for the better. This knowledge of communal power gives Buddy tremendous authority within his own community.

Junior, however, is isolated from the father that represents for him a sense of community, so the boy trembles on the edge of insanity. Buddy has an epiphany in which he recognizes that Junior's father is *in logos parentis* when he tells Mr. Pool that maybe they could hide Junior until his father gets home: "Buddy smiled. 'Maybe not,' he said. 'I figure his daddy won't make it home this week either'" (195). Even if there really is a Mr. Walter Brown living and working in New Jersey, for his son the man is nothing more than a fantasy, a verbal creation of the Symbolic Order with more reality in Junior's mind than in Junior's life.

At the end of *The Planet of Junior Brown*, it seems that Junior is beginning to heal. "The relative. . . . became less clear to Junior and somewhat fuzzy around his shoulder. The thing seemed to disappear part way into the wall" (217). The diminution of this mental construct of a male relative seems to fade in direct correlation to the nurturing Junior is getting from Buddy. Junior is able to begin murdering the fantasy-based relative because Buddy has provided him with an alternative to the destructive Oedipal triad of his home life. But although the possibility of Junior's growth is left ambivalent, Buddy's growth is clear; his development positions this novel as an *Entwicklungsroman*. He has grown because he has had surrogate father figures against which to rebel, and now he is free to be a father *in loco parentis* for the boys of his planet and Junior.

Two novels about girls placed in foster care after their mothers have abandoned them also delineate the creation and eventual abandonment of a parent figure created *in logos parentis*. In Katherine Paterson's *The Great Gilly Hopkins* (1978), Gilly constructs a mental image of her mother based on two postcards the woman has sent her proclaiming her love. Gilly rebels against her foster mother — a woman who acts *in loco parentis* — and gains for herself the power to move in with her grandmother. But when Gilly finally meets her mother, she is disappointed to discover that her biological mother does not love her. Gilly realizes that she has rejected the love of a genuine parent figure and that the rebellion she thought was liberating has in fact disempowered her. Her recognition of the power of the Symbolic Order is shattering, but she is at least able to murder her own construct, the mother she has made out of words, and go on with her life. The protagonist of *To All My Fans, with Love, from Sylvie* (1982), by Ellen Conford, is less self-aware about the implications of creating a parent for herself out of the Symbolic Order. Sylvie writes three letters to the mother she has never met during the process of running away from her foster father, who is sexually abusing her. When Sylvie returns into protective custody at the end of the novel, she has not recognized the role of language in her own self-delusions. She neither rebels against nor murders the *in logos parentis* figure she has constructed. As a result, Sylvie ultimately seems even more repressed than Gilly does.

In Lacanian terms, then, it is no mystery why an adolescent would construct a parent to murder out of the Symbolic Order: the child must come to terms with the Symbolic Order as a necessary precondition to understanding herself as a subject constructed of language. S/he must do battle with the Symbolic Order over the phallocentric obstacle to her/his desire in order to become an actualized subject (Lacan, *Écrits* 219–221). Inherently misogynistic and homophobic as some of Lacan's precepts are, they offer a unique way to read adolescent literature, for surely in fictional narratives even more than in "real life" (whatever that is) the construction of the Symbolic Order serves as a linguistic tool for analyzing the construction of the text. It is important to note that in all cases under discussion here, the adults who write these fictions have defined linguistic rebellion as essential to adolescents' empowerment. Such a message carries strong ideological implications.

### Ideology and Textual Authority

Since the characters constructing parents against whom to rebel are themselves the constructs of adults who exist outside of the text, YA novels serve both to reflect and to perpetuate the cultural mandate that teenagers rebel against their parents. So defined, the power dynamic between adolescents and adults is always already one of contested authority. But if YA novels are written even in small part to remind teenagers of their role in the site of contested authority, then issues of authority have ideological implications that bear further investigation. Such novels as Salinger's *The Catcher in the Rye*, Hinton's *The Outsiders*, Hamilton's *Arilla*

*Sun Down*, and Crutcher's *Staying Fat for Sarah Byrnes* convey their ideologies about authority through their narrative structure.

How a text expresses its ideology is a function of narrative structure. The level at which the ideology occurs affects the reader's perception of it. Peter Hollindale distinguishes explicit textual ideology from implicit textual ideology by asking us to investigate the messages the author intends to communicate in conjunction with those s/he communicates passively as "unexamined assumptions" (Hollindale, "Ideology" 10–15).[12] Hollindale does not clarify the obvious point that a text can communicate its explicit ideology either directly or indirectly: directly if the ideology is actually stated in the book; indirectly if the ideology is implied for the reader to infer. The distinction between explicit ideologies that the text directly articulates versus those that it only implies has repercussions for the power relationship that the text establishes with the reader. Unstated explicit ideologies left as inferences for adolescent readers to draw imply a different set of power differentials between the text and readers than explicit ideologies stated directly for readers' benefit. Indirect ideologies may, for example, imply that the reader has more knowledge or more capability to draw inferences than narratives that rely on directly stated ideologies.

The power dynamic also shifts if the ideological voice is stated by an adult voice rather than an adolescent voice. Some narratives that rely exclusively on adult voices to articulate direct ideologies may offer fewer affirmations of adolescents than texts that allow adolescents to have the power/knowledge necessary to engage with ideological statements. James Bennett's *I Can Hear the Mourning Dove* (1990), for example, is the story of two emotionally disturbed teenagers who help each other. They gain insights from each other rather than from some sort of omniscient adult. The ideology affirms teenagers' power, especially when it functions in community.[13] In order to better understand how such ideologies are communicated to readers, we can employ the strategies offered by narrative theory about the effect of narrative position and the relative involvement of a character in the role of narration. Narrative position affects the power dynamics involved in ideological communications within adolescent literature.

Gérard Genette has codified ways of investigating narrative position. His classification of various types of narrators demon-strates that the information to which narrators have access affects both the structure of a narrative and the narrator's role in the actual plot. In other words, textual knowledge empowers narra-tors. For example, a first-person narrator like Huckleberry Finn can only report on events to which he has epistemological access: he can only describe what he knows. Omniscient narrators like the narrative persona of *The Chocolate War* have access to more knowledge and therefore, arguably, access to more power than do first-person narrators like Huck Finn.[14] Far more important than how much information the narrator has is the issue surrounding how that information is used. Does the narrator use information to lead the reader to draw conclusions as Huck Finn does? Or does the narrator withhold information from readers that disables their deductive capabilities as occurs in *I Am the Cheese*? The knowledge a narrator has translates into various manifestations of power, depending on how the narrator shares that informa-tion with readers. Moreover, in adolescent literature, the power/ knowledge dynamic often underscores the didactic impulse of the narrative such that the narrative structure becomes tied to the em-powerment/repression dynamic that permeates the genre. Many of the first-person confessional narrators of the 1970s problem novel, for example, cannot resist the urge to tell the reader what they have learned. Mark's direct commentary to the reader about moral ambiguity in the last paragraph of S. E. Hinton's *That Was Then, This Is Now* (1971) comes to mind as one example: "I am too mixed up to really care. And to think, I used to be sure of things. Me, once I had all the answers. I wish I was a kid again, when I had all the answers" (154). Hinton makes sure that the reader knows Mark has learned that moral absolutes are difficult to de-fine. In this case, the narrator can be thought of as having power over readers because he is transmitting to them information that they may not have previously had.

Genette's codification of narrative position is helpful in de-scribing such relationships between the narrator and readers. He defines "author-narrators," those with a concept of the entire nar-rative structure, as "extradiegetic" narrators (229). Extradiegetic narrators are those who have a connection to the "public" in the way that they address their story to a reader who exists outside of their own story. Huckleberry Finn or the third-person narrator of *The Chocolate War* are extradiegetic narrators. They both have direct relationships with the reader of the narrative; both share their power/knowledge directly as the narrative unfolds. Interior narrators, on the other hand, are those with knowledge of only a portion of the narration; Genette calls them "intradiegetic" narrators (229). Intradiegetic narrators are interior narrators, characters who have knowledge of only a portion of the narrative.[15] As such, they have a direct relationship with their listening audience within the text but an indirect relationship with the actual reader of the text. Mr. Antolini, for instance, is an intradiegetic narrator in *The Catcher in the Rye* when he talks to Holden Caulfield about the difference between maturity and immaturity near the end of the novel. When Johnny writes Ponyboy a letter in *The Outsiders* telling his friend to keep being "gold" (154), Johnny becomes an intradiegetic narrator. He has a direct relationship with Ponyboy, just as Mr. Antolini does with Holden. But the reader of the book experiences Johnny's and Mr. Antolini's rhetoric through the filter of the extradiegetic narrator. Both *The Outsiders* and *The Catcher in the Rye* demonstrate how a narrator's relationship to the information in the text dictates the level of power s/he has: Ponyboy has more narrative authority and power than Johnny does, just as Holden has more narrative authority and power than Mr. Antolini does. Ponyboy and Holden control the reader in ways that Johnny and Mr. Antolini cannot.

Seymour Chatman's basic model of narrative structure proves useful here. The transmission process between author and reader moves through several levels of communication. Those in the box represent the text; the elements in parentheses Chatman identifies as fictive elements that are optional (151).

## Narrative Text

Real author → | Implied author → (Narrator) → (Narratee) → Implied reader | → Real Reader

Maria Nikolajeva analyzes this process at work in Aidan Chambers's novel *Breaktime* (1978). Chambers is the real author, Ditto is the implied author and the narrator of the text about his relationship with his father and his romance with Helen that constitutes the text of *Breaktime*. Ditto tells his story to his school chum Morgan, who serves as the narratee within the actual narration (Nikolajeva 195). The book then constructs an implied reader with its cultural references: the audience is meant to be white, middle-class, British, male, and adolescent. When I read the book, I am the real reader who may temporarily adopt the characteristics of the implied reader.

How a text expresses its ideology affects the construction of the implied reader. Most YA novels assume, for example, that the implied reader is adolescent. American YA novels tend to assume an American audience; novels by white Americans often assume a white audience. The implied reader of *The Outsiders* is one such case: the implied reader of that novel is a white American adolescent. With the assumptions that any text makes about what its reader knows, every text positions the implied reader in multiple subject positions.

A crisis in reading adolescent literature occurs, however, when the actual reader is displaced, when the subject position of the actual reader is violated.[16] Adult readers of YA novels accept the contract of reading outside their subject position when they pick up a YA novel. They know before they begin that they are reading against their subject position as an adult. Adolescent readers, however, might not expect their subject positions to be so violated, although female readers have so often been trained to read as male readers and black readers have so often been trained to read as white readers that they may not be uncomfortable with the disjuncture that necessarily occurs.[17] The relationship between the narrator and the implied reader often proves to be the crucible in which ideology is smelted in adolescent literature because the source of narrative authority in a text can reflect much about the text's ideology. Of special interest is the age of didactic characters who carry an adolescent text's ideology.

Most adolescent literature bears some sort of didactic impulse. In a literature often about growth, it is the rare author who can resist the impulse to moralize about how people grow. Adolescent literature is, therefore, rife with didactic explicit ideologies, however obliquely they may be worded.[18] *The Outsiders* is none too subtle in its message that class strife is both destructive and inevitable: the refrain "things are rough all over" (33, 103) echoes through the book. *The Catcher in the Rye* contains perhaps more subtle explicit ideologies, at least one of which is voiced by

Holden's teacher, Mr. Antolini, when he quotes, "The mark of the immature man is that he wants to die nobly for a cause, while the mark of the mature man is that he wants to live humbly for one" (188). In this case, an intradiegetic narrator voices the didactic ideology. The intradiegetic narrator is fairly removed from the narrative action and knowledge of the rest of the plot; it is Holden who knows what has happened in *The Catcher in the Rye*. But it is Mr. Antolini who knows what is happening — both to Holden emotionally and in the larger sense of what is happening to struggling adolescents in general. Mr. Antolini is serving *in loco parentis* to Holden. When Antolini becomes an authority figure, Holden's knowledge becomes at least temporarily displaced by Mr. Antolini's. In classic Freudian fashion, Holden rejects his father figure's advice, but the astute reader can recognize that it is the adult who is the wise one here. Holden, for all his rebellious ways respected by iconoclasts for decades, is not as smart as he thinks he is. In other words, Holden's narrative authority is undercut by the authority of an adult. *The Catcher in the Rye* assumes on one level a sympathetic audience, a reader who shares the narrator's awareness of high school politics and his prurient interest in sex. On that level, the implied reader of *The Catcher in the Rye* is an adolescent. This accommodation of an adolescent reader provides one explanation for the text's appeal to teenage readers. Yet when an adult assumes narrative authority within the text for the purposes of communicating an ideology of maturity, the adolescent implied reader is at least temporarily displaced.

The pattern is not altogether uncommon in adolescent literature. In Chris Crutcher's novels, wise therapists like the intradiegetic narrator Mr. Nak in *Ironman* (1995) dispense wisdom for the emotionally shattered characters in the novel, including the extradiegetic narrator, teenage athlete Bo Brewster. When Mr. Nak communicates *in loco parentis* with an air of authority about how Bo can manage his anger, Nak is an adult narrator temporarily displacing the adolescent implied reader. In Angela Johnson's *Toning the Sweep* (1993), the extradiegetic narrator's grandmother, Ola, teaches her to accept death in a passage in which she takes on the role of intradiegetic narrator (88–90). Ola concludes that her granddaughter must be allowed to take risks in order to live. The imagery is very similar to Holden's epiphany in *The*

*Catcher in the Rye* when he decides to let his sister reach for the brass ring on a carousel: "The thing with kids is, if they want to grab for the gold ring, you have to let them do it, and not say anything. If they fall off, they fall off, but it's bad if you say anything to them" (211). This passage contains the key to Holden's growth: he must accept change. But he achieves his epiphany only after he has heard Mr. Antolini's message about risk taking. At least temporarily, all of these characters lose narrative power to alternate narrators who usurp their authority within the text for a time. It is as if these characters and the implied readers they are addressing must lose authority for a while to an adult, usually a parent figure, to gain personal power by the end of the narrative.

Virginia Hamilton's *Arilla Sun Down* offers one more layer of complexity to this model because she adds questions about the nature of social construction to this novel's ideological discourses. On the surface, Hamilton's *Arilla Sun Down* is a novel about sibling rivalry. Arilla Adams and her older brother, Jack Sun Run Adams, are the children of an African American mother and a Native American father. Arilla and her brother are engaged in a continual power struggle. She spends most of her life thinking her brother wishes her dead because his actions toward her range from the negligent to the malicious. But Jack's antipathy is only part of why Arilla feels excluded from both her family and her community. For one thing, the other children in town are not sure what to make of her because few of them come from homes as happy or as privileged as hers. For another, they are not sure what to make of her race. One child even exclaims, "I didn't know they was for-real Indian. . . . I thought they was just passing" (67). Hamilton problematizes the spectrum of race quite intricately in this novel; she acknowledges not only interracial tension, but intraracial tensions among African Americans who call Arilla "light-skinned. . . . because even now they can't bring themselves to say black out loud, since they already spent so much time hating the word and what it stood for" (30). These same people also view Arilla's Haitian girlfriend critically. Arilla must learn how to negotiate a position for herself within this race-conscious community, and she learns that skin color certainly affects social power in her culture.

Arilla also feels keenly her difference from the rest of her family. She wishes she had the charisma her parents and brother have

(42, 49) and asks, "Who am I? Why do I have to be the ugly one?" (114). Jack exacerbates Arilla's sense of exclusion by claiming only his Amerind heritage, as he prefers to think of himself, and by denying that she is of "The People," as their father would say (20). Jack Sun Run derisively calls her "Moon" to assert his masculine dominance over her and identifies her as black because she looks more like their mother than he does. In thus rejecting his own black heritage (and his mother), Jack implies that being Native American (and male) is preferable to being African American (and female). As long as Arilla accepts the position Jack assigns her of being out of touch with her Amerind identity, she feels powerless. But Arilla eventually learns that he is wrong on several counts: first, she is as much a "blood" as he is, just as he is as black as she is, and second, neither race is better than the other; they both just *are*. In making this decision, she quits rejecting both her mother and her father and embraces the support they have to offer her. Finally, Arilla learns that she is as strong as Jack is, regardless of their genders.

Arilla comes to her questioning of her racial identity while she is writing her autobiography for a school assignment. Although the assignment seems to play only a small part in the story, its metaphorical value turns out to be enormous, for Arilla's primary identity formation centers around her burgeoning awareness of the Symbolic Order as she comes to define herself as a storyteller. This self-consciousness about storytelling foregrounds discursive practices in the text because Arilla can only come into her own as a writer when she explores both her conscious and her subconscious knowledge of racial discourse. Thirteen-year-old Arilla publicly communicates her conscious knowledge of racial discourse in the nine chapters she narrates as the text's first-person extradiegetic narrator. Three of the chapters, however, are narrated from her subconscious memories of events that happened when she was five. Since as a thirteen-year-old she does not remember these events, these chapters are more private than those that seem to be chapters of her public autobiography; they are also narrated in a completely different voice that marks how Arilla holds competing subject positions as an African American and a Native American. As a five-year-old, she narrates the book's opening lines: "Late in the big night and snow has no end. Taking

me a long kind of time going to the hill. Would be afraid if not for
the moon and knowing Sun-Stone Father is sledding" (1). In contrast, her first lines that she narrates as a teenager read, "For sure,
my Birthday would be a disaster. I mean worse than the time they
tell about when that Learjet piloted by some rock-and-roll star-
boys crash-landed in Wilson Onderdock's Black-Angus pasture a
mile outside of town" (18). The narrative distance the character
feels from the events she narrates in these two sections also serves
as a commentary on Arilla's sense of alienation: Arilla experiences
separation not only from her community, but she is also separated
from some of her own empowering memories. The narrative dis-
junction that occurs between Arilla's split voices represents how
devastating fragmentation is: as long as Arilla cannot remember
her past — that is, as long as part of her memory is exterior to her
own consciousness — she cannot find a place in her community
and must remain exterior to it.

The disjointed "rememories" (14) of Arilla's fifth year focus on
her friendship with an Amerind couple who call her "Wordkeeper" (173), identifying her as a tribal storyteller. The two of
them are the private, intradiegetic adult narrators who are also this
text's Ideology keepers. They serve *in loco parentis* to Arilla as she
gradually enters the Symbolic Order. They are the parents she effectively kills; she does so by disremembering them once she has
entered the Symbolic Order. The father figure, James Talking
Story, pronounces the text's ideology of race: "One time there are
blue-red-yellow birds, but all are one bird. There are black-brown-
white horses, but all one horse. It is so with all things living. So
with all trees and men. White, brown, black, yellow. Red. Once,
only red men. But not now. Now, all. *All*, with peace" (87). In
James's discourse, race is masculine. His partner, Susanne Shy
Woman, states the text's gender ideology in discourse that also
sublimates race to gender: "nobody knows what the reservation
been doing to the women. No woman ever sign a treaty I know
of, and maybe that's the reason a treaty never hold together" (91).
I rather suspect that the women do, in fact, know what the reservation is doing to them; Susanne's "nobody knows" assigns
knowledge to men, regardless of their race. In any case, it is two
intradiegetic adult narrators serving as temporary parent figures
who articulate this text's ideologies about race and gender.

As a thirteen-year-old, Arilla must integrate into her consciousness what she learned as a five-year-old about being a Wordkeeper
before she can come to terms with her racial heritage and her
gender. One act serves to clarify both terms of her confusion.
When her brother is injured during an ice storm, she saves his life
in an act he considers one of "counting coup" (216). It is the first
time in their relationship that she takes a leadership role, and she
does so by relying on her repressed memories of herself as one of
The People. She successfully rides her horse through the storm,
sensing that she is surrounded by spirits, "things all around, I can
feel them" (199). Since she talked to James's spirit after he died
when she was five, the reader may conclude that it is James Talking
Story's spirit who is helping her again. She conquers her fears and
saves her brother when she ceases to rebel against James as her
father figure and shares authority by accepting the tribal knowledge he offers her. Arilla renames herself "Arilla Sun Down" after
this experience, at once acknowledging that her brother does not
dominate her and that she is simultaneously African American and
of The People. Discursive and ideological knowledge give Arilla
power.

Once she accepts what Henderson would call the "plural aspects of self that constitute the matrix" of her subjectivity (18),
Arilla recognizes that her tribal role as Wordkeeper is a public role
for people of all races and genders. She no longer feels like an
outsider to her own family or her community, and as a result, she
makes her most powerful discovery about storytelling: "Maybe
that is writing, changing things around and disguising the for-real"
(247). Words are the ultimate source of power for her because they
are the means by which she explores what truth is. Arilla discovers
this for herself, and in accepting her role as storyteller, feels that
she understands her place in her community and in her family.
Nevertheless, it is still adults who first hold the ideological truths
that Arilla must learn. The point is even linguistically verifiable
within the text's discourse: "truth" is Arilla's father's favorite in-
terjection (21, 62, 233, 234, 235, 239), but Arilla does not appropriate this word, this Name-of-the-Father, for her own diction
until after she has renamed herself "Arilla Sun Down," that is,
until after she has learned the truth about herself and become
more of an adult, more of an insider to the communities she be-

gins to claim as her own (209, 231). But she does not wield this power until she has been the narratee of two adults' ideological lessons for her.

In *Arilla Sun Down*, *The Catcher in the Rye*, *Toning the Sweep*, and *Ironman*, adults hold the knowledge that represents the highest goal: truth. No adolescent is given the opportunity to be as wise. The only way teenagers can obtain that goal is to grow, to quit being adolescents themselves, to become more like the insiders, the adults. But if that is the case, by that formulation young adults automatically become outsiders in their own novels. I am often surprised by the number of YA novels that imply the same ideology to adolescent readers: stop being an adolescent and become an adult. Perhaps S. E. Hinton was more broadly accurate than even she knew when she named her first novel *The Outsiders*.

Wisdom is, by its very nature, the province of adulthood; children learn from adults because adults often do know more than adolescents — although authors like Virginia Hamilton, Chris Crutcher, Robert Cormier, Madeleine L'Engle, and Cynthia Voigt are always scrupulous about depicting at least some smart teenagers and some adults who know far less than the adolescents around them. But when James Talking Story knows more than Arilla or Mr. Antolini knows more than Holden Caulfield, it is difficult to determine whether adults are teaching adolescents or reinforcing their lack of knowledge. Are the adults emphasizing the adolescents' powerlessness, or are the adults nurturing the adolescents so as to eventually empower them? Are these novels an example of adults appropriating the position of power, or are they simply reflecting a reality that allows adolescents to grow? The answers probably lie somewhere on the spectrum between these two polarities because, as Foucault points out, power can be both repressive and enabling; it is from within the confines of powerlessness that people rebel and discover their own power (*History* 36–49; *Discipline* 195–228). Thus, if Mr. Antolini is temporarily appropriating Holden's power, it is possible that this repression is one avenue that will eventually force Holden to discover what means of power are available to him. Perhaps Holden must necessarily be the object of Antolini's didactic impulse in order to grow. Like all teenagers, Holden must experience powerlessness as a necessary condition of growing into power.

Peter Hollindale argues that adolescent literature is by definition a literature about transitions; that in providing examples of epiphany that serve effectively to instruct adolescents about their potential, the literature serves as a bridge between childhood and adulthood (*Signs* 116–131). Thus, Hollindale might conclude that the tension between the positioning of the adolescent and the adult in YA literature is a function of the genre's transitive nature. YA novels are teaching adolescents how to become adults because that is their function. Hollindale's explanation is very tolerant of — and even explains — the didacticism in the literature. According to his view, teaching adolescents about growth is the whole point.

But whatever else we conclude, whether we decide that the power transactions between adolescents and adults in YA literature are heinous, enabling, or inevitable, the fact remains that the discursive practice of employing a wise adult to guide a confused adolescent is so commonplace in adolescent literature that it is practically invisible even to many trained readers. Take Chris Crutcher's *Staying Fat for Sarah Byrnes* as an example. On the most superficial level, *Sarah Byrnes* is a sports novel about successful competitive swimmers. Far more important, the novel can be classified as what Hollindale would call an "adolescent novel of ideas" because of its unflinching look at a variety of controversial topics, including abortion, child abuse, and religious tolerance ("Adolescent" 86). The first-person narrator, called "Moby" because he is fat and a swimmer, is friends with Sarah Byrnes, whose face has been intentionally burned by her abusive father. Sarah's mother has abandoned her family out of fear of Mr. Byrnes's monstrosity; Sarah is temporarily devastated when she discovers that the mother she has created for herself *in logos parentis* will not defend her against Byrnes's attacks. One level of the narrative action involves how he is finally brought to justice by Carver Middleton, an accountant who dates Moby's mother. The other narrative line shows how a self-righteous evangelical Christian named Mark Brittain learns to become more tolerant of both religious difference and his own imperfections when he eventually faces his responsibility in his girlfriend's abortion. The adolescent characters are connected through Ms. Lemry, the swimming coach and teacher of a course called Contemporary American Thought.

Ms. Lemry is one of the three adult characters involved in directly articulating this text's explicit ideologies. Mr. Ellerby, an Episcopalian minister who helps Brittain gain some measure of self-forgiveness, makes direct statements about the importance of the separation of church and state, religious tolerance, and recognizing our own imperfections (171, 198). Carver Middleton, the accountant turned vigilante who brings Mr. Byrnes down, condemns the Vietnam War and affirms the importance of recognizing our personal social responsibility (211). His words about social responsibility contribute to the text's dialogics about abortion, religion, and changing society. The astute reader can ultimately conclude that Crutcher advocates individual social involvement, whether or not we are guided by religious faith. Coach Lemry serves as the third adult who carries the burden of the narrative's ideology. She even adopts Sarah Byrnes by the end of the novel, affirming her authority *in loco parentis* quite substantively.

The Contemporary American Thought course that Lemry teaches serves as an arena for showcasing many of the text's explicit ideologies. She insists that students learn to be respectful of divergent opinions and that they are accountable for their actions in her class. She even teaches them that ideology is relative when she tells them, "No issue is isolated. . . . because our *points of view* — the way we perceive things — are inextricably linked to our beliefs" (98, emphasis in the original). At this point in the novel, Moby still controls the narrative as the extradiegetic narrator. But in chapter 17, when Ms. Lemry narrates the story of how she and Sarah Byrnes have confronted Sarah's mother, she becomes an adult intradiegetic narrator assuming narrative authority. During that passage, Lemry communicates indirectly but explicitly a key ideology in this novel of ideas: adults are responsible for protecting children. The assertion is one I believe so firmly that it feels to me like Truth rather than ideology. Nevertheless, it is a sentiment that I recognize as one that directs power away from adolescents and toward adults. It also raises an interesting question about the implied reader of this novel. Is it adolescents who most need to learn the lesson that adults are responsible for protecting their children? Or is it adults who need to learn that lesson?

How the implied reader is positioned in a text helps us to understand some aspect of the multivariate relationship between power and ideology in adolescent literature. Crutcher's *Staying Fat for Sarah Byrnes* is ostensibly pitched to adolescents and yet much of the text's explicit ideology is pitched to adults. Many textual references, moreover, are coded to appeal to Baby Boomers, hardly the age group meant to be reading a YA novel published in 1993. Crutcher's references include Raymond Burr, William Conrad, Perry Mason, Bob Dylan, Buddy Holly, the Byrds, the Dave Clark Five, the Turtles, Alex Haley's *Roots, The Stepford Wives*, the Son of Sam, Edgar Bergen, and the Lovin' Spoonful (3, 11, 23, 36, 79, 91, 102, 106). Ostensibly, the narrator is a fan of sixties and seventies music because his mother buys him one CD of music recorded between 1956 and 1975 for every more recent one he buys, but the only contemporary music the text references is a mention of one character's Twisted Sister T-shirt. Perhaps by employing cultural references Crutcher considers classic, he is avoiding the problem of "evanescence" that Caroline Hunt describes existing as a liability for YA novels: cultural references in teen culture change every few years, rendering any book that describes pop culture in contemporary terms obsolete in a few years (5). Or perhaps he is out of touch with teen culture. Either way, the net result of a phrase like the reference to one character's having "a zeal rivaled only by Alex Haley's relentless search for Kunta Kinte" is the possible alienation of adolescent readers. Taken together with the fact that the majority of the novel's explicit ideologies are articulated by adult characters, the Baby Boomer-directed allusions in *Staying Fat for Sarah Byrnes* would seem to have a high potential for displacing the adolescent implied reader.

Whenever I read a novel that seems to preclude the possibility of an adolescent reader who can fully apprehend the text, I begin to wonder about the purpose of adolescent literature. Is *Staying Fat for Sarah Byrnes* simply a failed novel because of the cultural gaps? Or is it just more direct about the relationship between the adolescent and the adult than most Anglo-American YA novels? Are its time-bound allusions simply a result of Crutcher's chronological age? Or is it possible that he is foregrounding an inherent tension in the genre that requires us to question the very purpose of the genre? If this last is true, perhaps Crutcher is implying that the ultimate purpose of adolescent literature is to teach adolescents to quit being adolescents. If that is the case, the genre is indeed a dark one. Jacqueline Rose might even call it "impossible" in the same way that she calls children's literature inherently contradictory because of "the impossible relation between adult and child. . . . Children's fiction sets up a world in which the adult comes first (author, maker, giver) and the child comes after (reader, product, receiver). . . . Children's fiction sets up the child as an outsider to its own process, and then aims, unashamedly, to take the child *in*" (1–2, emphasis in the original). Since the necessity of growth is foregrounded even more often in adolescent than children's literature, perhaps YA novels are even more "impossible."

But I prefer to think of them as paradoxical. Although children's literature is capable of celebrating "childness" — the characteristics associated with childhood (Hollindale, *Signs* 44–48)— adolescent literature seems to delegitimize adolescents, insisting that "adolescentness," especially immaturity, is unacceptable, even though the surface intention of most YA novels is ostensibly to legitimize adolescence. Texts accomplish this delegitimization by conveying frequently to readers the ideological message that they need to grow up, to give up the subject position culturally marked "adolescent." In order to mature, they need to murder the parent who represses their power, regardless of whether that parent is actual, surrogate, or imaginary, so that they can fully enter into the Symbolic Order. Since so many adolescent novels contain parents who must be rebelled against and adult narrators who are the source of the text's often repressive ideological wisdom, the genre does seem to communicate to teenagers that authority is not and should not be theirs. In communicating such ideologies to adolescent readers, the genre itself becomes an Ideological State Apparatus, an institution that participates in the social construction of the adolescent as someone who must be repressed for the greater good.

### CHAPTER 4

## *"All of a sudden I came"*

### SEX AND POWER IN ADOLESCENT NOVELS

The protagonist of Norma Klein's *It's OK if You Don't Love Me* (1977) experiences orgasms easily. Twice she climaxes "all of a sudden" (78, 142), which is in marked contrast to the protagonist of Judy Blume's *Forever* (1975), who says, "at last I came" (149–150). For both girls, reaching their sexual potential feels truly potent. The same is true in the obverse for male characters in Robert Cormier's *The Chocolate War*, who experience powerlessness as impotence. When Jerry Renault perceives himself as a J. Alfred Prufrock, unable to disturb the universe, he is incapable of achieving climax (93). Sexual potency is a common metaphor for empowerment in adolescent literature, so the genre is replete with sex. Teenage characters in YA novels agonize about almost every aspect of human sexuality: decisions about whether to have sex, issues of sexual orientation, issues of birth control and responsibility, unwanted pregnancies, masturbation, orgasms, nocturnal emissions, sexually transmitted diseases, pornography, and prostitution. The occasional teenage protagonist even quits agonizing about sexuality long enough to enjoy sex, but such characters seem more the exception than the rule. But for many characters in YA novels, experiencing sexuality marks a rite of passage that helps them define themselves as having left childhood behind.

Typically, sexuality as a rite of passage is linked with romance in YA literature. Romantic YA novels follow a relatively predictable pattern, demonstrated by such novels as Virginia Hamilton's *A White Romance* (1987), a book that consciously plays on the romance tradition. Generally speaking, two teenagers feel sexually attracted to one another in a standard YA romance. The action is occasionally blocked during a stage in which each character thinks the attraction is unrequited. The characters eventually communicate and express their attraction. Then the action is blocked while they make decisions about consummating their passion. More often than not, they express their passion with some sort of sexual contact. In *A White Romance*, two characters named David and Talley are so consumed by their passion that they have sex on the kitchen floor in a friend's apartment. And then — in *A White Romance*, as in most YA romances — all hell breaks loose. One character or the other regrets the action or betrays the other or ends up pregnant, creating what proves to be the most extended conflict in the book. (In *A White Romance*, David uses racial politics to manipulate Talley.) After the conflict is resolved — Talley, in this case, quits dating David and starts to date instead a classmate who respects her — the protagonist ends up sadder and wiser, and the reader has been exposed to a very direct ideology: sexuality is powerful and can hurt people. Although nonromantic YA novels about sexual victimization like Voigt's *When She Hollers* (1994) and Block's *The Hanged Man* (1994) do not follow the predictable made-for-TV patterns replicated in books like Zindel's *David and Della* (1993) and Hadley Irwin's *Abby, My Love* (1985), they do still share the same ideological message that sex is more to be feared than celebrated.

As a result, adolescent literature is as often an ideological tool used to curb teenagers' libido as it is some sort of depiction of what adolescents' sexuality actually is. Adolescents certainly do not have one shared sexuality or even share common opinions about sexuality, but many YA novels seem to assume that the reader has a sexual naïveté in need of correction. Some YA novels seem more preoccupied with influencing how adolescent readers will behave when they are not reading than with describing human sexuality honestly. Such novels tend to be heavy-handed in their moralism and demonstrate relatively clearly the effect of adult authors asserting authority over adolescent readers. Moreover, adolescent novels that deal with sex, whether they are obviously ideological, usually contain within them some sort of power dynamic wherein the character's sexuality provides him or her with a locus of power. That power needs to be controlled before the narrative can achieve resolution.

As a topic, then, sexuality in YA novels often includes a lesson for the reader to learn, and the topic also illustrates how language controls our perceptions of a bodily function. In other words, sexuality is inseparable from language; it is influenced by and even constructed by the words that people think and say. Thus, sexuality in this genre is discursive and ideological. To illustrate the ideological nature of sexuality in YA novels, I will first employ Michel Foucault's theories to assess didacticism at work in several novels that focus on heterosexual teenagers, including Judy Blume's *Forever*. Second, an examination of *jouissance* illustrates Foucault's depiction of the relationship between knowledge and power in creating sexual pleasure; Madeleine L'Engle's *A House Like a Lotus* (1984) proves especially useful in examining these issues. Finally, books about male and female homosexuality surface cultural assumptions about the discursive nature of sexuality. Aidan Chambers's *Dance on My Grave* (1982), Francesca Lia Block's *Baby Be-Bop* (1995), M. E. Kerr's *Deliver Us from Evie* (1994), and Nancy Garden's *Good Moon Rising* (1996) are books that tie the discursive nature of sexuality to the power/repression dynamic at work in much of adolescent literature.

## The Ideology of Sexuality

In contrast to "sex," which is a purely biological act, Foucault defines "sexuality" as a discursive construct (*History* 68–69). That is, sexuality is influenced by, even created by, language. Although his critics have decried the ways that this definition denies the prediscursive physicality of human sexuality, Foucault's notions of the discursive quality of sexuality are particularly useful in analyzing sexuality in literature, where every action is, quite literally, always already and only constructed by language.[1] According to Foucault, Western cultures have separated sexuality from sex as a way to regulate it. Sex is the biological action in Foucault's economy; sexuality is the all-encompassing mores and discourses that have arisen to define and regulate human sex acts (*History* 33–35).

Foucault's *The History of Sexuality* demonstrates that regulating sexuality is central to the ways that Western cultures define themselves. He suggests that far from being on the verge of being liberated by discourses of sexuality, Western cultures are dependent on a definition of sexuality as repressed. Western discourses about sex are repressed, he argues, because any number of institutions from the Catholic Church to Freudian analysis have gone to ingenious lengths to create monumental rhetorical systems (such as confession as sacrament or psychoanalysis) that depend on people talking about sex. The result is a social obsession with sexuality: "What is peculiar to modern societies, in fact, is not that they consigned sex to a shadow existence, but that they dedicated themselves to speaking of it *ad infinitum*, while exploiting it as *the* secret" (*History* 35).

Foucault also thinks of human sexuality in terms of two things: discourse and power. He asserts that in Western culture, sexuality depends on a power/repression dynamic: sex is so powerful that it must be but cannot be controlled. In contrast to Eastern cultures that base their attitudes about sexuality on notions of pleasure to create an *ars sexualis*, Western cultures have developed an entire *scientia sexualis* founded on the relationship between discourse and knowledge to increase the (forbidden) pleasure of sexuality, Foucault observes, and this "regime of power-knowledge-pleasure . . . sustains discourse on human sexuality in our part of the world" (*History* 11). This relationship between power and knowledge is grounded in discourse: "Indeed, it is in discourse that power and knowledge are joined together" (*History* 100). The specific pleasure of toying with the discourse of sexuality is grounded in the desire to at once control and exploit sexuality:

> We have at least invented a different kind of pleasure: pleasure in the truth of pleasure, the pleasure of knowing that truth, of discovering and exposing it, the fascination of seeing it and telling it, of captivating and capturing others by it, of confiding it in secret, of luring it out in the open — the specific pleasure of the true discourse on pleasure. (*History* 71)

These two beliefs — that the power/repression dynamic surrounding sexuality has led to the creation of a discourse that pretends to cloak but actually exposes sexuality and that knowledge and pleasure are woven inextricably into the fabric of that discourse — lead Foucault to theorize that Western ideas about sexuality depend on notions of deviance to define what is allegedly mainstream or normal. In many YA novels, teenage sexuality is defined in terms of deviancy — even when the message to the reader is a Judy Blume special: "Your masturbating/wetdreams/ desire to have sex/(fill-in-the-blank) is normal."[2] Such novels reflect cultural norms that tend to define teenage sexuality in terms of deviancy in an attempt to control adolescents; nonetheless, reassurances to teenagers that their actions are normal still start from the assumption that someone thinks their actions are not.

Judy Blume's *Forever* is a classic in this genre. As seventeen-year-old Katherine decides to have sex, the narrative sends the reader conflicting messages that demonstrate Foucault's principle that Western cultures at once liberate and repress sexuality. The text of *Forever* has an obvious explicit ideology: it is normal for teenagers to want to have sex. Moreover, Blume seems to have written *Forever* as a self-help manual to help teenagers learn more about sex: the book describes having vaginal examinations (138–139), how to get birth control (chapters 14 and 15), a basic description of penises (85), condom usage (113), premature ejaculation (114), impotence (167), sexual relations during menstruation (70), venereal disease (104), experiencing a broken hymen (115), premarital pregnancy (154–155), giving a baby up for adoption (179), and a play-by-play description of how to have intercourse (149–150). The text tries to liberate teenage sexuality by communicating that curiosity about sex is natural, but it then undercuts this message with a series of messages framed by institutional discourses that imply teenagers should not have sex or else should feel guilty if they do.

For example, in Katherine's first heavy-petting session with her boyfriend, Michael asks her if she is a virgin. She says she is and tells him, "Well, now you know," to which he replies, "Don't get defensive, Katherine. It's nothing to be ashamed of" (28). At one level the dialogue could be criticized for its lack of verisimilitude: it is hard to imagine a teenage boy who has been fondling his girlfriend on a sofa for an hour being coolly analytical as he says of her virginity, "It's nothing to be ashamed of." But even more important, the dialogue can be criticized for its hypocrisy, for the language is couched in institutional discourse with rhetoric ostensibly about patriarchal attitudes toward girls' chastity that are thinly disguised reinforcements of those values. I read those words and cannot help thinking, "Shame never crossed my mind until Michael said no one should be ashamed." The passage reminds me of an injunction against thinking about pink elephants: we cannot help it once we have been told not to. Katherine has internalized the institutionalized sanctions against sex, which becomes clear when she later thinks, "Even though I know it's natural and I'm glad my parents love each other I can't help feeling embarrassed," when she overhears their lovemaking (58–59). *Forever* doth protest too loudly: the reader may learn to feel shame about sex from being told not to feel ashamed.

Several institutional voices are implicated in the deconstructive ideologies at work in *Forever*. Katherine mentions that she has received sex education from school, from her parents, and from her grandparents. In fact, Katherine's grandmother is a lawyer who advocates freedom of choice; she counsels her granddaughter early and often about making wise choices with her sexuality:

"Just be careful . . . that's my only advice."
"Of what?"
"Pregnancy."
"Grandma!"
"And venereal disease."
"Really . . ."
"Does it embarrass you to talk about it?"
"No, but . . ."
"It shouldn't."
"But listen, Grandma . . . we aren't sleeping together."
"Yet," Grandma said. (43–44, ellipses in the original)

Katherine's grandmother encourages her to go to the Margaret Sanger clinic to get birth control, and her parents have designated the family den as the appropriate place for her to bring dates rather than going parking because "it isn't safe, not because of anything we might do, but because there are a lot of crazies in this world and they have been known to prey on couples who are out parking" (26). Her mother tells her, "It's up to you to decide what's right and what's wrong . . . I'm not going to tell you to go ahead but I'm not going to forbid it either. It's too late for any of that. I expect you to handle it with a sense of responsibility though . . . either way" (93, ellipses in the original). On the one hand, Katherine has a strongly defined matriarchal support-system, but on the other hand, her mother and grandmother both construct intercourse in terms of something that requires emotional and physical protection, implying Katherine's vulnerability.

Katherine's mother gives her an article that typifies the text's confused ideology. Called "What about the right to say 'no'? Sexual liberation" and authored by "the director of medical clinics at Yale" (120), the article asks its readers to consider whether intercourse is necessary to their relationship, what they expect of it, where they can seek help, and whether they have "thought about how this relationship will end" (120). The final question upsets Katherine with its implication that all teen relationships end. The article implies that teenage sexuality is therefore suspect because it rarely occurs within permanent relationships. The author of the article is clearly someone who disapproves of the concept of "sexual liberation."

The whole of *Forever* carries the same message: kids are freer about sex than they were prior to the 1970s, but they still end up getting hurt. In this discourse, sexuality is at once liberated and repressed. For example, Katherine is hurt when her relationship with Michael ends because she is attracted to another male; Michael seems even more hurt than she is by their breakup. In another example, Katherine's friend Erica pressures a thinly disguised gay male to have sex with her; his inability to do so leads him to attempt suicide. Another friend, Sybil, gets pregnant and says, "I could have had an abortion but I wanted the experience of giving birth" (180). Her callowness comes back to haunt her, however, for she has more trouble giving the baby up for adoption than she had imagined. These teenagers may be enjoying their sexuality, but the consequences are devastating to them, and Blume wants the reader to know that.

The mixed message about repressing and liberating sexuality is frequently grounded in this text as it is in many YA novels in gender politics. Such texts as *Forever, Edith Jackson* (1978), and *My Darling, My Hamburger* (1969) imply that sexual liberation is a good thing, but that it is the girl's job to make sure that male sexuality is not so liberated that she becomes victimized.[3] When Michael tells Katherine to enjoy her physical impulses, she says, "I have to control my body with my mind" (57) and "I don't like to lose control of myself" (84); she is the one who tells him when they need to stop (27, 73). Katherine is the apotheosis of control: she is a young woman who not only never forgets to make her bed but who also cannot even imagine how anyone else would forget (146). She defines herself in terms of control — but is complicitous in her boyfriend's inability to control himself.

The double standard about sexuality is reinforced by the objectification of women that occurs in this book. Pleasing men seems to be Katherine's highest goal. She wears light blue on their first date because she "once read that boys like light blue on a girl better than any other color" (23). Katherine criticizes her mother's "flabby thighs" (29, 177), and she accepts Erica's explanation that Katherine's father is overprotective because he is just being Freudian (63). When she is going skiing with Michael, Katherine teases, "How can I get buried in an avalanche with Michael watching out for me?" (66). And when Katherine wants to be on top during their lovemaking one night, he calls her "aggressive" (186). She seems to recoil, "I hadn't thought about that until he said it. I was surprised myself. 'Do you mind?'" (186). Of course he doesn't — but the fact that so much is made of how unusual the situation is defines what "normal" intercourse should look like for teenage girls. The astute female reader has much to learn from this ostensibly liberating book about how to be a "good" (read: "repressed") girl.

One thing *Forever* tries to do right is to depict Katherine having orgasms. It may be unbelievable that she has them at all, but at least Blume commits herself to depicting female pleasure. But the scenes in which she does are oddly clinical and lack detail:

> He rolled over on top of me and we moved together again and again and it felt so good I didn't ever want to stop — until I came.
>
> After a minute I reached for Michael's hand. (85)

> I let my hands wander across his stomach and down his legs and finally I began to stroke Ralph [Michael's penis].
>
> "Oh, yes . . . yes . . ." I said, as Michael made me come. And he came too.
>
> We covered up with the patchwork quilt and rested. (111, ellipses in the original)

> This time Michael made it last much, much longer and I got so carried away I grabbed his backside with both hands, trying to

push him deeper and deeper into me — and I spread my legs as far apart as I could — and I raised my hips off the bed— and I moved with him, again and again and again — and at last I came. I came right before Michael and as I did I made noises, just like my mother. Michael did too. (149–150)

No doubt Blume felt the need to circumscribe her descriptions of Katherine's pleasure lest the book be censored even more than it already is, but it is hard to think of a book being sexually liberating when it has such a heavy-handed ideological agenda and when it is so dispassionate in depicting female *jouissance*.[4] Katherine sums up the book's ideology in the final passage: she thinks she was ready to love Michael and to have sex, but she is not ready for a permanent commitment. "I think it's just that I'm not ready for forever" (220). Given that so much of the book has been dedicated to communicating to teenagers that they should not have sex outside of committed relationships, that final message does seem to contradict Katherine's loud declamations about her self-confident assertion of her sexuality.

Teaching adolescents to repress their liberated sexualities is a recurring theme in the *Entwicklungsromane* of the late 1960s and early 1970s. Many of the novels in this genre define themselves in terms of sexual dilemmas, but they share a moral tone sanctioned by the dominant culture. Undoubtedly, it is the undercurrent of disapproval about liberated teenage sexuality that allowed these books to get past the de facto censorship of YA publishing. Books like Paul Zindel's *My Darling, My Hamburger* and Rosa Guy's *Edith Jackson* show teenage girls who are hurt by their own lack of self-control: both books depict teenage girls who get abortions. Zindel condemns the character he creates who has an abortion, whereas Guy applauds her character, who decides not to give birth to an unwanted child, but regardless of whether their agendas are pro-life or pro-choice, both books imply that promiscuous sex in the first place is the real problem. Beatrice Sparks's *Go Ask Alice* (1971) ties sex to drug abuse: the narrator of the journal ends up prostituting herself to buy drugs. Although the ideology is clearly antidrug, the book contains an implied message that the worst thing that can happen to a teenage girl is her own self-commodification of her sexuality. W. Keith Kraus pointed out in 1975 that too many problem novels are ideologically heavy-handed when he wrote, "the sexual act itself is never depicted as joyful, and any show of intimacy carries a warning of future danger" in these novels (22). Sex leads to disaster for many adolescent characters.

Ironically enough, Judy Blume claims to have written *Forever* as an antidote to these type of books:

> I wrote the book *Forever...*, when [my daughter] was fourteen.
> She asked if I could write about two nice kids who fall in love,
> do it, and nothing terrible happens to them. Randy had read a
> number of books that year that linked sex with punishment. If
> a girl succumbed she would wind up with a grisly abortion,
> abandonment and a life ruined. I think Randy was bothered
> by the message of those books in which boys never had any
> feelings and were only interested in using girls. And neither
> boys nor girls ever felt responsible for their actions. (*Letters to
> Judy*, 204)

In Blume's haste to communicate about sexual responsibility, however, her book becomes as didactic as those she condemns. It proves ultimately impossible for her to write a novel about teenage sexuality without linking the story to societally sanctioned ideologies.

The same could be said more than twenty years later, for even when novels like Block's *Weetzie Bat* (1989) and Sparks's *It Happened to Nancy* (1994) describe sexuality, they still carry the unavoidable ideological overtones of the dominant culture. *Weetzie Bat*, for example, is predicated on the notion that sexual expressions of love are good, whether they are expressed between people of the same or opposite sexes. But Block cannot escape the trappings of our culture: writing within a post-AIDS culture, she only sanctions sex that occurs between committed, loving couples in permanent relationships. Block's books carry no more approval for promiscuous sex than do Blume's. Weetzie, in fact, gets beat up and date-raped when she does not carefully guard her sexuality in a blaming-the-victim scene early in the novel: "Weetzie glimpsed the handcuffs for a second before Buzz had her down on the mattress. She kept her eyes on the bare bulb until it blinded her" (12). The next day a friend notices the "tattoo-like bruise" Buzz has given her and forbids her to see him anymore (13); the text is vague about whether Weetzie ever would have figured out for herself that her relationship with Buzz has been self-destructive.

*It Happened to Nancy* is an even clearer case of blaming the victim: Nancy is date-raped by a conniving pederast and then dies of AIDS in a dramatically short period of time. Although the text directly tells any reader who has been the victim of a rape "YOU WERE NOT RESPONSIBLE" (223) and although Nancy's mother tells her daughter, "it wasn't my fault, that I shouldn't blame myself," Nancy still thinks she is ultimately responsible for being a sexual victim: "If a kid wants to do some crazy thing, she'll find a way. Like me — cutting school and stuff" (34). Nancy's boyfriend echoes her Victorian sexual attitudes:

> He told me that when his parents had said that they were going to divorce, right then and there he made a commitment, solemn as it could be, that he would never have sex until he was married. He had heard that word *sex* over and over between his parents, and even though he was only ten and didn't really understand what sex really meant at that point, he knew it was the thing that had destroyed the family. His dad was having sex with other women, and with his mom sick and all, it was really dreadful, *dreadful, DREADFUL!* (65–66, emphasis in the original)

Beatrice Sparks — so-called editor (but I assume author) of both *Go Ask Alice* and *It Happened to Nancy*, although they are both marketed to teenagers as anonymously written diaries — has the same agenda in 1994 as she does in 1973 in *Go Ask Alice*. She wants girls to stay in control of their sexuality so that they do not get hurt. The goal may be admirable, but it comes at the cost of stigmatizing all sexuality.

Similarly, Chris Crutcher seems to have the best of intentions in *Running Loose*. Louie Banks and his girlfriend Becky ski to a secluded cabin, intending to spend the night, and Louie decides he is not ready to have sex, so they don't. Although Louie is a virgin, Becky is not; she has had at least one other lover. Crutcher's intent to communicate to macho guys that they do not need to force their sexuality on anyone to prove anything is commendable — except in the way that it reinforces notions that males are predatory and women are vulnerable. That Becky dies in a car wreck soon after this scene reinforces both characters' vulnerability. It is as if she has to die for being a scarlet woman and he has to atone for his sin of making her the object of his lust by losing her forever.

Realistically speaking, we live in a society that objectifies teen sexuality, at once glorifying and idealizing it while also stigmatizing and repressing it. Foucault might argue that adults enjoy lecturing to adolescents about sexuality because it gives the adult power and a certain sexual pleasure, the scintillation present in the act of forbidding. For one thing, the adult holds the power, becomes the dominatrix as it were, and for another thing, the adult has the opportunity to discuss the forbidden in that circular pattern of mentioning the unmentionable that Foucault demonstrates typifies Western discourses about sexuality. The adultism YA authors hold in this situation is formidable.

I would also add that the adultist power these authors hold is very much tied to gender politics. Male and female authors alike who communicate that sex is to be avoided to protect vulnerable females ultimately end up affirming the patriarchal status quo, no matter how good their intentions. Until the unlikely day when Western cultures can define sexuality in terms of *jouissance* instead of repression, discourses about adolescent sexuality are likely to remain stultified in this Möbius strip of denying sexual pleasure and then deriving pleasure from discussing that denial.

At this point, I can imagine many people — especially parents — asking me if I am actually proposing either divorcing sex from ideology or even worse, advocating that teenagers engage in promiscuous sex. I cannot say that I am, although I would prefer to live in a culture with entirely different values regarding sexuality. What I am proposing for the here and now, however, is that parents and teachers and librarians and literary critics take serious looks at the ideological intent behind most of the YA novels published with the seeming intent of validating teenagers' self-assurance about human sexuality. Most YA novels about teenage sexuality have at best a conflicting ideology and at worst a repressive ideology that both reflects and perpetuates Western culture's confused sexual mores. But the very existence of these repressive ideologies demonstrates that sexuality is a locus of power for adolescents. If it were not, adults would feel no need to regulate teenagers' sexuality.

## Sex and Power/Knowledge/Pleasure

Nothing demonstrates the power relationships between adults and teenagers as effectively as the abuse of sexual power. Novels about incest, for example, demonstrate the misappropriation of adult power over the nonadult body of a child or adolescent: Hadley Irwin's *Abby, My Love*; Block's *The Hanged Man*; Voigt's *When She Hollers*; Grimsley's *Dream Boy* (1995); and Chbosky's *The Perks of Being a Wallflower* (1999) depict the emotional repercussions for children sexually abused by parent figures. Each of these novels revolves around the necessary precondition of an adult who is capable of turning a child into an object. In each case, sexual pleasure and sexual knowledge are the provenance of the adult perpetrator rather than the child victim. And each of these books contains at least some possible bibliotherapeutic potential for readers. Especially in the case of *The Perks of Being a Wallflower* and *The Hanged Man*, the child victims learn they have power over their own voice: they can overcome their victimization only by talking about it. It is significant that these texts communicate to readers that victims can have some form of power. Ultimately, the incest survivors in these novels learn about repression and empowerment, but only because their bodies have been completely disempowered at some point in their lives.

On the opposite end of the spectrum are novels in which teenagers celebrate their sexuality free from both adult repression and victimization. In novels as diverse as Aidan Chambers's *Breaktime* and Madeleine L'Engle's *A House Like a Lotus*, teenagers derive pleasure from their increased knowledge of sexuality. Their subsequent sense of empowerment illustrates Foucault's principle of the power/knowledge/pleasure dynamic: characters who have positive experiences with sexuality are usually strengthened by the experience. Authors who depict teenagers experiencing extreme sexual pleasure also tend to minimize the repressive use of ideology.

In *Breaktime*, for example, Aidan Chambers is unusual in depicting a heterosexual scene from a male perspective that allows for female sexual agency and does not devolve into didacticism. Both characters seem empowered by their sexuality. Here, modified from the original style to facilitate the restrictions of academic style, is an excerpt from the climax of the book, the prose poem section in which the protagonist, Ditto, describes a sexual encounter:

> Her hands ran down my chest, across my stomach. Found the clasp of my jeans. Undid it. Drew down the zip. Pushed jeans and pants below my knees. . . . She pulled at me, turning me over upon her, urgently, as she fell back upon the ground. And gave me entrance with a deep delighting sigh. And then there were no more words no more thoughts Nothing but movement body on Flesh on flesh on Mouth and hands and legs and thrusting driving wild relief felt during her high long scream. (158–162)

The sex scene proves to be a rite of passage for the protagonist, Ditto. After he has sex, he is able to empathize with his father for the first time, which implies that sex is what makes him a man. Although that in itself seems a somewhat dubious premise and a reinforcement of patriarchal ideology, at least Ditto and Helen have enjoyed their shared sexual experience and neither ends up diseased, pregnant, emotionally devastated, or dead. In a strategy unusual for this genre, Chambers allows the teenagers power that is predicated on pleasure and knowledge of that pleasure.

Norma Klein's Jody Epstein and Lyle Alexander enjoy their sexuality and work together to ensure that they both achieve pleasurable orgasms in *It's OK if You Don't Love Me*. For all that Jody is a bit neurotic and self-obsessed, her openness about sexuality, learned from her mother, is refreshing. In a particularly Freudian turn of events, she experiences her first orgasm during intercourse after she and Lyle have defeated her father and another man at tennis. Once Jody feels more powerful than her father, she is finally free to experience her own *jouissance*.

Several feminist authors depict sexual pleasure by relying on some form of female sexual *jouissance*, that is, by allowing their characters to experience intense sexual pleasure that appears to carry the subject beyond language. In Cynthia Voigt's *On Fortune's Wheel* (1990), Birle and Orien come together "as a man does to a woman" and Birle is "not surprised to find in herself a hunger that matched his" (241). The text only implies her *jouissance*, but when she eventually bears his child, no stigma is attached to her fertility. In fact, she rejoices at having a daughter, chooses to raise the child on her own, and eventually reconciles herself to Orien's permanent presence in her life when he abdicates his kingdom to live with her and their daughter.

Ursula K. Le Guin's *The Beginning Place* (1980) contains a scene of sexual *jouissance* more direct than the one depicted in *On Fortune's Wheel*, but as in that fantasy novel, the sexual climax follows the characters' triumph over the force of evil with which they have been in conflict. Hugh and Irene have just slaughtered the terrible creature that holds Tembreabrezi hostage:

> He held her to him, but awkwardly and timidly, until she put up both her arms, feeling herself go as soft and quick as water. Then he held her and mounted on her, overcoming; yet her strength held and contained his strength.
>
> As he entered her, as she was entered, they came to climax together, and then lay together, mixed and melded, breast against breast and their breath mingled, until he rose in her again and she closed on him, the long pulse of joy enacting them. (169–170)

Le Guin takes pains in this passage to depict both characters' sexual pleasure. That a "pulse of joy enact[s]" them implies that their orgasms have some sort of reifying power to actually create something else altogether new, although Hugh is the subject and Irene the object of the construction, "as he entered her, as she was entered" (169). At least neither character ends up dead, pregnant, or abandoned.

In *A House Like a Lotus*, L'Engle also seems to know instinctively that the pleasure/knowledge/power dynamic is integral to our understanding of human sexuality. At sixteen, the protagonist, Polly, is the eldest of seven children. An eccentric and rich artist named Max befriends her, giving Polly new insights into artistic culture and multiculturalism. Max is a complicated woman. After the death of her baby daughter, Max and her husband divorced, and Max established a permanent relationship with a surgeon named Ursula. When Polly first learns that the woman she has idolized is a lesbian, she reacts with a homophobia common among teenagers in the 1980s. The girl tells herself that her anger is a result of Max's dishonesty, but the woman has never lied to Polly, so the reader infers Polly's extreme homophobia. Polly's fear demonstrates two loci of power: Max has hurt Polly and Polly, in rejecting the friendship for a time, hurts her friend. That dual loci exist becomes more important when later in the novel Max gets drunk and makes sexual overtures to Polly. Polly runs away, horrified, hurt, and disgusted by Max's hypocrisy: Max has already condemned her own father for sexually molesting his daughter, Max's sister. Since Max has repeatedly positioned Polly as her daughter figure, the overture has such strongly incestuous overtones that Polly almost permanently ends their friendship.

Much of the rest of the novel deals with the lessons Polly learns about forgiveness. Max immediately recants in complete self-abnegation. She is aware that she has abused her power in this situation — but presumably, that was part of what made it exciting to make a pass at Polly in the first place. The sexual predator thrives on having power over a victim, and in this scene in which Max bases her need for physical contact with Polly on a need for "an affirmation of being," Max is predatory (187).

> In the next flash of lightning she stood up, and in the long satin gown she seemed seven feet tall, and she was swaying, so drunk she couldn't walk.
>
> And then she fell . . .
>
> I rolled out of the way. She reached for me, and she was sobbing. (187, ellipses in the original)

Polly eventually forgives this breach of trust in part because of her knowledge that Max is dying of a fatal tropical disease. If Max has the power to establish a mother-daughter relationship and then victimize her daughter figure, Polly also has power in this relationship: she elects to be a daughter figure, but she refuses to be victimized. Eventually, it is she who has the power to maintain the relationship because she holds the power to forgive her transgressor.

But another way that L'Engle depicts Polly's power is with an unusual expression of female *jouissance*. After Polly flees from Max's unwanted sexual advances, the girl goes to the home of a medical intern she is dating named Renny. Her decision to have sex with him is undoubtedly tied to her own need to affirm her heterosexuality, but the passage is nevertheless the most poetic rhetoric in the book:

> Gentle. Not frightening. Knowing what he was doing. I felt my nipples rise, and it startled me.
>
> "Shhh," Renny whispered. "Shhh, it's all right, don't worry, just relax and listen to your body."
>
> He was slow, rhythmic, gentle, moving down my
> body, down . . .
> and I was nothing but my body
> there was a sharp brief pain
> brief
> and then a sweet spasm went through me
> and I seemed to rise into the air
> no more pain
> just the sweetness
> the incredible
> oh, the
> and then Renny, panting
> I pressed him hard against me. (260)

L'Engle's effort to portray the ineffability of *jouissance* captures something of the division Foucault tries to maintain between sex and sexuality, with "sex" being the physical action and "sexuality" being the cultural forces (including language) used to regulate it. The separation is, of course, an artificial one, as L'Engle's use of language to depict a lack of language demonstrates. Language is inseparable from the action, as she well knows.

L'Engle also uses language to assert Polly's agency in this scene. Polly may initially be the object of Renny's sexual advances and she may be having sex with him out of her homophobic fear of Max's sexual overtures, but the teenager nevertheless claims a subject position with respect to her own body. She asserts her agency during intercourse when she describes her nipples rising, then her whole self rising, and again when she portrays herself in the subject position during the completion of their lovemaking : "I pressed him hard against me" (260).[5] L'Engle's careful articulation of Polly's sexual agency is an even stronger feminist statement than her celebration of *jouissance*. Polly knows the power of her sexuality because she perceives herself as an agent in the process rather than as an object, as happens with so many female characters in YA novels. Polly's pleasure, therefore, is based on her knowledge of her own power.

Two friends Polly makes in Greece serve as foils to Max in demonstrating that a young woman can have some choice and therefore some power in her sexual relationships. Polly makes friends with a bourgeois American teenager who tries to seduce her. She eventually sees through his posturing when he puts both of their lives at risk and she saves them from drowning. From this point on, she refuses the sexual power he has over her because she recognizes that sharing her sexuality with him would be self-destructive. As in her relationship with Max, Polly has the power to define the level of intimacy the two will share. Another friend Polly makes, named Omio, has witnessed the abuse of power that colonizing missionaries have had over the people in his homeland, a Polynesian island. Omio teaches her that he has forgiven his oppressors because "My father told me we must learn to love such people, because they must be sick in their minds, and only love could heal such sickness. When people have great power, lo, they become very sick, and must be loved as we love those who are dying" (256). But he also teaches Polly that people who are sexually attracted to one another can still have chaste friendships. Polly feels physically drawn to Omio and feels shame when she discovers that he is married. They decide to remain friends, and Polly finds a certain serenity in learning that she can have a powerful and platonic relationship that does not engage her sexuality. This knowledge makes it possible for her to forgive Max: only after she learns that she can love Omio without acting on her sexual impulses does she trust Max's promise that her mother figure will never again act on her inappropriate sexual impulses.

L'Engle does not shy away from depicting the power of human sexuality in relationships that may or may not appropriately include sexuality. Max has had consensual relations with both her husband and her lover, but she is sexually drawn to her daughter figure as Max's father was drawn to his daughter. Polly has intercourse with a man ten years older than she and is sexually attracted to a married man. Yet she refuses to have sex with two people: her mother figure and the narcissistic boy whom she knows will hurt her. Ultimately, every configuration in the novel in which sexual attraction is not mutual is depicted as destructive. If L'Engle has an ideology it is not that female sexuality is destructive but that sexual victimization is. The message may be a liberating one for adolescent readers accustomed to the stigmatization of teen sexuality, especially female sexuality.

Whether a novelist writing for adolescents depicts sexuality as a matter of pleasure or displeasure, however, the depiction itself is usually a locus of power for the adolescent. Characters who have explored their sexuality usually learn something from the experience, which is why sex is a rite of passage in so many adolescent novels. This tendency to link sexuality with maturation has a certain didactic impulse to it: as long as the adolescent learns something from the experience, then the literary representation of sexuality seems more acceptable within a genre dedicated to teaching adolescents how to become the Other — an adult. Ultimately, the connection between sexuality as a site of power, knowledge, and pleasure proves to be one more occasion for ideological indoctrination in the genre.

## Queer Discourse

Nonheterosexual teen romances employ a different set of ideologies that are meant to empower queer teenagers.[6] Although novels about gay males and lesbians are often more different than they are alike, they share a tendency to address how teenagers are affected when they develop their sexuality oppressed because of their orientation. This oppression of queerness exemplifies one obvious site of power being limited in adolescent literature. The novels are also revelatory for the ways that they highlight a physical act — sex — being transformed by discourse into sexuality, which Foucault insists pervades the culture (*Power* 190; *History* 106).

Such YA novels about gay males as Aidan Chambers's *Dance on My Grave* and Francesca Lia Block's *Baby Be-Bop* are very Foucauldian in their tendency to privilege the discourse of homosexuality over the physical sexual acts of gay men, defining homosexuality more rhetorically than physically. Themselves entirely constructed by language, these novels fall prey to the same chicken-and-egg dilemma that plagues Foucault's work: which comes first, the body or the word? In and of itself, this paradox would not necessarily be problematic except for the fact that all too often the rhetoric these texts employ to construct gay discourse is more repressive than liberating.

Homosexuality, of course, is one of the many aspects of sexuality that Western institutions such as the church and psychoanalysis have defined as abnormal in an attempt to control this unwieldy force that is human sexuality (Foucault, *History* 42–44). But because power and repression are such fluid constructs, eventually "homosexuality began to speak in its own behalf, to demand that its legitimacy or 'naturality' be acknowledged, often in the same vocabulary, using the same categories by which it was medically disqualified" (*History* 101). Although Judith Butler has criticized Foucault for minimizing the importance of sexual difference (*Gender Trouble* xxii, 31), queer theorist Jonathan Dollimore notes that at least Foucault's identification of homosexuality as a discursive construct was one of the factors that helped Euro-American culture move beyond thinking of being gay only in terms of binaries like "normal" and "deviant" (179). As Foucault explains discursive constructs such as sexuality, "There is not, on the one side, a discourse of power, and opposite it, another discourse that runs counter to it. . . . there can exist different and even contradictory discourses within the same strategy" (*History* 101–102). This, then, is what I wish to explore in this section: queer discourse in young adult literature creates contradictory discourses because of the way sexuality is defined by the relationship between power, knowledge, and pleasure. The characters' physical pleasure is often undermined by their knowledge of homophobia, so their ability to enjoy their sexual power is limited.

The male adolescent character who has sexual contact with another male in a YA novel illustrates clearly the Foucauldian concept that sexuality is informed by the relationship between discourse and power because many gay YA male novels use a gay character to illustrate how the issues of pain and pleasure inherent in human sexuality are discursively formed. Together, pain and pleasure fashion a matrix of power in which each of the gay characters in these novels functions. Even when authors depict teenagers who are aware that discourse fashions their sexuality, these authors self-censor their gay male characters. What gay and lesbian YA novels tend to demonstrate, then, is the limits of queer discourse at work in adolescent literature: as a group they show how a genre can become more self-aware of a social issue without necessarily providing the reader with progressively transformative experiences.

Christine Jenkins's "Heartthrobs and Heartbreaks: A Guide to Young Adult Books with Gay Themes" is an annotated bibliography of gay and lesbian novels published from 1969 to 1988. Although Jenkins does not analyze discursive tensions in these novels, she does classify the stereotypes to be found in the first twenty years of gay YA literature as she sees them: the stereotypical YA gay male is financially secure, attractive, and white; he lives on one of the coasts, loves the arts, has a troubled family, and has difficulty recovering from the loss of his first love. His sex acts are rarely described with any kind of detail; that is, he is often denied physical pleasure (82–85). I might add that he is often an only child: three of the four principal gay male characters in the novels under discussion here have no brothers or sisters, which reinforces their isolation. Jenkins cites John Donovan's *I'll Get There. It Better Be Worth the Trip.* (1969) as the first YA novel to treat gay issues openly. This novel certainly fulfills all of the stereotypes that Jenkins identifies, plus a few more, not least of which is that the protagonist, Davy, has an overbearing, alcoholic mother who does not understand him. In other words, his family is troubled almost entirely because of his mother's narcissism; the novel implies that Davy's mother has somehow driven him to homosexual sex.

Aidan Chambers's *Dance on My Grave* perpetuates some of the same stereotypes: one of the gay characters has a terrifically overbearing mother; both gay characters are white, middle-class, single children. The novel, however, uses discourse that celebrates gay pleasure to a certain degree. But as its title indicates, the book is more about death than about homosexuality, despite its Library of Congress designation "[1. Homosexuality — Fiction. 2. Death— Fiction]." Being gay is not Hal Robinson's problem (in the sense of the typical problem novel, which this book most emphatically is not); grief over the death of Barry Gorman, Hal's lover, is. Nevertheless, the pain and pleasure of sexuality are discursive issues in this novel because Hal is a character fascinated with language.

The starting point of *Dance on My Grave* is Hal's explanation to a court-appointed social worker in his hometown, a British seaside resort named Southend, about why he was arrested for desecrating Barry's grave. Hal and his lover made an oath before Barry's death that whoever survived would dance on the other's grave. Hal writes the story both as an explanation to his social worker and to mitigate his grief. Several passages demonstrate his awareness that he — and everyone — is discursively formed: he discusses with one of his friends that "we invent the people we know. . . . Perhaps we even invent ourselves" (246). The epigraph from the first chapter is a quotation from Kurt Vonnegut's *Slaughterhouse-Five* that focuses the reader's attention on this point: "We are what we pretend to be, so we must be careful what we pretend to be." Moreover, Hal tells his social worker that the process of writing his story has been more important than actually living it: "I have become my own character. . . . Writing the story is what has changed me; not having lived through the story" (221).

Hal knows that discourse is power. And he also knows that discourse and knowledge are inseparable. As Kirk Fuoss notes, Hal is Foucauldian in recognizing that "desire . . . not only precedes but also exceeds language" (171). Hal is frustrated by his inability to put his knowledge of his desire for Barry into words. In the early stage of his romance with Barry, Hal comments that verbalizing their feelings reifies their relationship; it only becomes real once they have discussed it: "knowledge is power. Once somebody knows that about you — knows how you *really* feel about them — once you've declared yourself, then they know about you, have power over you. Can make claims on you" (83). It is the act of enunciation — not the act of sex — that gives the relationship ontological status.

Sex with Barry does bring Hal physical and emotional pleasure, however, and the discourse of the novel is very direct in communicating that. Falling in love with Barry satisfies the "desire for a bosom buddy" Hal has felt since he was seven years old (44). Chambers does not shy away from describing the boys' first kiss or their frequent caresses, although in keeping with the unwritten publishing codes that dominate the production of YA literature, the adolescents' genital sex acts are alluded to only interstitially. But at least Hal's euphemisms are humorous; when they finally have genital contact, Hal quips, "[Barry] gave me a present from Southend. Wish you were here?" (149). Even so, Hal implies that the emotional pleasure he takes from their relationship is far more important to him than are the sex acts. He lovingly describes their conversations and their activities:

> all I knew for certain was that I couldn't get enough of him. I wanted to be with him all the time. And yet when I was with him that wasn't enough either. I wanted to look at him and touch him and have him touch me and hear him talk and tell him things and do things together with him. All the time. Day and night. (155)

But eventually Barry reacts to Hal's obsessive pleasure in their relationship, telling Hal: "It's not what we do together that you want. It's me. All of me. All for yourself. And that's too heavy for me, Hal. I don't want to be owned, and I don't want to be sucked dry. Not by anyone. Ever" (179). They are Barry's last words to his lover. Within an hour Barry dies in a motorcycle accident. Hal's pleasure has been Barry's pain; now that pleasure is transformed into Hal's own pain.

One major purpose of *Dance on My Grave* is to communicate that obsessive love is not healthy, regardless of one's sexual orientation. But Chambers also communicates both that sexuality is inseparable from a pleasure/pain dynamic and that discourse is power. It seems to me that Chambers knows his Foucault well. Nevertheless, *Dance on My Grave* contains an almost Calvinistic series of messages about homosexuality. For example, Hal spends more time describing his first lover as "cactal and overpowering" than he does describing his own physical or emotional pleasure (51). And even though Hal never expresses remorse, shame, or even confusion about being gay, he is still forced to dress as a girl and pose as Barry's girlfriend if he wants to see his lover's body in the morgue; Hal is still denied a photograph of his lover by Barry's mother, who — not incidentally — has an "overactive Id" (35); he is still arrested for fulfilling his oath to his lover when he dances on Barry's grave. And worst of all, his father almost certainly perceives his sexual orientation as pathological: "I can hear in the tone of [my father's] voice: he was saying, 'What I think you need the doctor can't do anything about'" (240). Perhaps these scenes in the novel accurately reflect what it meant to be gay in the 1980s, but it does seem to me unfortunate that despite Chambers's affirmative rhetoric about being gay, he still focuses more on Hal's pain than on his pleasure. But at least Hal denies neither the reader nor himself knowledge about how central his orientation is to his identity.

As in *Dance on My Grave*, Francesca Lia Block's *Baby Be-Bop* self-consciously constructs sexuality as a discursive process, but then, given how metafictional all of Block's novels are, this is no real surprise. The story is a prequel to *Weetzie Bat*; in it, Weetzie's friend Dirk comes to understand and accept his sexuality. Dirk and his best friend, Pup, love each other deeply, but Pup homophobically rejects his obvious feelings for Dirk and abandons their friendship. Dirk — like so many gay YA protagonists — feels far more pain than pleasure in this novel, although he never denies his knowledge of the pleasure he takes in his orientation.

After Pup's rejection, however, Dirk falls into a tailspin that culminates in a painful near-death experience. As he lies ill, the genie in his grandmother's lamp (the same one who grants Weetzie her three wishes in *Weetzie Bat*) shows Dirk his forebears' stories. He learns that his great-grandmother had his grandmother, Fifi, out of wedlock; he learns about Fifi's love for her husband and of his parents' consuming passion for each other. Each of these three embedded narratives is a symphony of the relationship between pain and pleasure for those who love: Fifi's husband, for example, knows he is dying, so he directs all of his love to her and ignores their son, who subsequently grows up not knowing how to love his son until after his own death. The ghost of Dirk's father urges the boy to be different, not to give up on life (or his sexuality) when it causes him pain:

"I want you to fight. I love you, buddy. I want you not to be afraid."

"But I'm gay," Dirk said. "Dad, I'm gay."

"I know you are, buddy," Dirby said. And his lullaby eyes sang with love. "Do you know about the Greek Gods, probably Walt Whitman — first beat father, Oscar Wilde, Ginsberg, even, maybe, your number one hero? You can't be afraid." (86)

Dirk is an unusual character in that he can come out to his parents without shame, an important discursive act of enunciation in a YA novel. Moreover, since myth is entirely language based and the three historical figures Dirk's father names are all writers, the catalog of gay forefathers that Dirk's father lists provides Dirk with a heritage that is discursively situated. But the power of his father's acceptance is somewhat attenuated by the fact that Dirk can come out to his father only after the man is dead.

Despite this, the novel promises Dirk happiness: the genie shows him the future and the hope of his relationship with Duck. Dirk's pleasure with Duck may be deferred, but at least he will have it eventually: "When they first kiss, there on the beach, they will kneel at the edge of the Pacific and say a prayer of thanks, sending all the stories of love inside them out in a fleet of bottles all across the oceans of the world" (103–104). Dirk and Duck's love — and their sexual pleasure — is treated as sacred in this text.

In the most metafictional passage of the text, Dirk asks the genie why he has appeared. The genie answers:

Think about the word destroy. . . . Do you know what it is? Destory. Destroy. Destory. You see. And restore. That's re-story. Do you know that only two things have been proven to help survivors of the Holocaust? Massage is one. Telling their story is another. Being touched and touching. Telling your story is touching. It sets you free. (104)

The "ye shall know the truth and the truth shall set you free" theme is blatant, but in a genre that tends to suppress positive homosexual discourses, this openness is welcome.

But the pain-pleasure matrix surrounding being gay is still complex in this narrative. Dirk's father, for instance, characterizes homosexuality in terms of fear, in terms of repression, not in terms of passion or pleasure or freedom. The most important message he has for Dirk is not to fear. Although that may be a message all adolescents — and especially gay/lesbian ones — need to hear, it is not exactly a joyous proclamation or even very positive rhetoric. Moreover, although the text affirms Dirk's orientation, *Baby Be-*

*Bop* never shows him engaged in a loving relationship; readers have to refer back to *Weetzie Bat* before they can read about Dirk and Duck's relationship. The only positive gay sex enacted in this novel occurs in Dirk's vision of his future with Duck. Before Duck meets Dirk, "he never talked to the men he touched in bathrooms and parks and cars. Is this what it means to be gay? Duck wondered. He missed the clean, quiet beaches of Santa Cruz," even though he has left Santa Cruz because it is such a homophobic community (100–101). Block sends a clear message that gay sex is not acceptable unless it is accompanied by love. She separates the physical act of "sex" from "sexuality" as a discursive construct in what Foucault considers typical Western fashion (*Power* 190; *History* 106). Human sexuality explored within a relationship is far more acceptable in this novel than the simple act of sex by itself is. But since sexual love can be painful and pleasurable whether it is homosexual or heterosexual, perhaps Block is simply being realistic.

The rhetoric begins to seem ominous, however, when the genie compares homosexuality to the Holocaust. The discourse is reminiscent of Hal's father implying that his son needs to be "cured" in *Dance on My Grave*. Block and Chambers have fallen into the language of pathology. Bergman notes that "all three of the ways in which patriarchy has conceived of homosexuality — as sin, crime, and disease — place it within frameworks that deny it permanence since sins may be overcome, crimes avoided, and diseases cured" (37). Chambers's and Block's rhetorical choices imply the perpetuation of such patriarchal notions even while they try to communicate to readers that being homosexual is not a disease, not a simple matter of choice, not a matter of victimization. So why the rhetorical choices evoking pathology? It seems virtually impossible for YA authors — even those with the best intentions — to escape from the hegemony of heterosexist discourse.

Lesbian YA novels display some of the same tendencies, especially in the way that they interrogate discourse by raising the question of audience. Are such books as M. E. Kerr's *Deliver Us from Evie* intended for lesbian readers? For straight readers? For female readers? For all readers? Elizabeth A. Ford notes the tendency of some literary critics to assume that books about the lesbian or gay teenager "are only for those *directly* (physically?) involved in the issues" (132, emphasis in the original). Moreover, if the text describes gay or lesbian acts, they are usually described in language that endeavors to normalize them. That is, the texts strive to reassure readers that gay or lesbian sex is not toxic or abnormal or even unusual. The very fact that the text implies that the act *needs* normalizing carries with it the same ideological implication that institutional discourses prohibiting heterosexual teenage intercourse carry: that which is already societally sanctioned, chastity, hardly needs normalizing.

Vanessa Wayne Lee therefore classifies lesbian novels into three categories. Stories that assume that lesbianism needs to be normalized and so seem to be glorified informational books she calls "education" texts (154), those that explore "the formation of lesbian identity" (152) she calls "coming-out" books (154), and those that "interrogate received wisdom about lesbianism and lesbian identity" (152), she calls "postmodern" for the ways that they "decenter, while problematizing, issues of information and identity" (158). These last are more likely to be marketed to adults than adolescents and so are beyond the scope of this current study. Lee's classification system, however, is useful in providing a paradigm for investigating how the discourses of pain and pleasure are manipulated by cultural discourses in novels with heterodox ideologies that are marketed to teenagers.

M. E. Kerr's *Deliver Us from Evie* falls into the category that Lee describes as educational (152) in that it attempts to normalize lesbianism by defining it in nonthreatening terms. The book is narrated by Parr Burrman, an adolescent farm boy who describes his sister Evie's coming out. Adult perceptions serve as the source of stereotypes that need correcting throughout the novel. For example, Evie's mother nags her to wear more feminine clothing. Eventually, Mrs. Burrman acknowledges that changing Evie's exterior will not change her interior, although as a mother, she still wishes her daughter would not perpetuate stereotypes about lesbians. Mrs. Burrman also suspects that Evie's lover is a lesbian because her mother is an alcoholic. Moreover, Mr. and Mrs. Burrman think that their daughter's lesbianism is a phase, and their farmhand, who wants to marry Evie so that he can control the farm, delegitimizes lesbianism when he says, "it's not serious enough to be a sin. It's kid stuff. Two women is . . . Now two men — that's another matter. That's sin in the Bible" (101, ellipses in the original). Presumably, Kerr hints at the man's eroticization of lesbianism in what Lee refers to as a typical heterosexist tendency to consider lesbianism "as a facet of male heterosexual pleasure" (152). But the farmhand is an adult who, like the narrator's parents, constructs lesbianism either in terms of its being transitory or its being pathological.

The narrator disagrees with his girlfriend's attempts to paint lesbianism as morally wrong when she attributes local flooding to God's wrath invoked on those who support lesbians. Evie's strongest statement describing her lesbianism reads: "I know you so-called normal people would like it better if we looked as much like all of you as possible, but some of us don't, can't, and never will! And some others of us go for the ones who don't, can't and never will" (86). Her proclamation confirms the ideology "that lesbianism exists, whether the reader . . . likes it or not" (Lee 154). Ultimately, the narrator parallels his love for his girlfriend with Evie and Patsy's love; the text concludes with a predictably formulaic theme that love is love, no matter what. This is an attempt at normalizing lesbianism that operates by flattening the differences between hetero- and homosexual relationships. Kerr's inability to depict lesbianism in terms other than "see, it's just like being straight" undermines her good intentions of instructing readers to perceive all the stereotypes perpetuated in this book as wrong.

Evie's initial discussions about her lesbianism revolve around the utterance of the concept "lesbian." Only once Evie self-identifies as lesbian, only when she proclaims her queerness and annunciates and affirms her identity, does she begin to seem happy. Moreover, she tells her parents to disregard other people's utterances about lesbianism, saying that she admires a lesbian singer precisely because "she doesn't care what people say about her" (57). Moments later she tells her father, "I don't give a ding-dong-damn what people say about me" (58). Evie understands the importance of language, especially the importance of not giving other people power to diminish her with their words. Later, Patsy Duff's father threatens the Burrmans with legal sanctions, implying that Evie and Patsy's relationship breaks laws about leading minors astray. Mr. Duff intuitively knows that more is at stake than a physical relationship, so he seeks protection from the threat he feels by invoking a legal system that codifies sexual behavior. Evie and Patsy reject his discursive, authoritarian attempt to regulate their sexuality when they run away to New York. Despite engaging numerous stereotypes — or even, perhaps, because it is so stereotypical — *Deliver Us from Evie* demonstrates how human sexuality is inevitably regulated by discourse, such as legal or religious rhetoric.

*Deliver Us from Evie* attempts to educate the reader that lesbianism is not external, it is not a phase, it is not the result of bad parenting, it does not exist as a function of serving male erotic pleasure, it is not a sin. The novel also functions within cultural assumptions about the power of language to regulate a physical activity. But the one thing *Deliver Us from Evie* fails to do is to indicate any source of lesbian pleasure. Evie's poetry about her lover is described, but the legitimacy of her eroticism is not (although her brother's is, in a heavy-petting scene with his girlfriend). *Deliver Us from Evie* is thus representative of a whole category of books in which lesbian knowledge of sexual power is as divorced from pleasure as it is in many books about heterosexual *jouissance*.

If *Deliver Us from Evie* is an educational novel about lesbianism, Nancy Garden's *Good Moon Rising* is a lesbian coming-out novel. Jan and Kerry fall in love while working on a production of *The Crucible*. Jan thinks of their first kiss, "as if she were waking out of a long sleep into something new and wonderful — scary too" (76). But their sexual contact has brought the two girls both joy and power, "[Jan] felt suddenly elated, strong, powerful. . . . with Kerry beside her, with Kerry having touched her, kissed her" (77). Garden does not avoid describing their first kiss or subsequent sexual contact in some detail: "Jan touched Kerry gently wherever Kerry touched her, wanting to feel what Kerry felt as well as what she herself felt; it was as if her body had been waiting for this all its life and hers, as if it were suddenly coming alive on its own. It was wonderful and terrifying at the same time" (147). Jan's Cartesian mind/body split captures something of the duality inherent in Foucault's identification of the Western separation between sex and sexuality. Her body feels things her mind can only reflect upon as if it were not participating, as if it were possible for her body to experience sexual excitement without any influence from her brain. Moreover, she has internalized contradictory feelings about her sexuality: the power she feels is both pleasurable and frightening.

Jan and Kerry explore their lesbian identities and decide they are comfortable with them — until they are outed by their peers. At this point, the book begins to interrogate the construction of lesbianism in ways that allow for its eventual celebration. The two girls do not proclaim their orientation until after they have publicly disavowed it. But because knowledge of their lesbianism brings both Jan and Kerry pleasure, they eventually affirm that pleasure in front of their peers and feel as a result more fully empowered. Jan quits lying about her orientation at a party when she tells her friends, "I *am* gay," and she feels stronger immediately: "With the words came a sense of relief and liberation so great that she felt she never wanted to hide again, even though she knew at the same time that she might have to" (221). Garden's text captures succinctly the dual nature of sexual pleasure that Foucault identifies: Jan refuses and accepts repression in the same sentence. Language, not physical activity, determines Jan's sense of identity. Lesbianism, then, in this novel is as discursively informed as it is in *Deliver Us from Evie*.

Queer YA novels often imply that they will engage in a discourse with bibliotherapeutic intent: readers — queer, bisexual, or straight — should feel a sense of catharsis or validation or acceptance of homosexuality after reading such novels. The assumption seems to be that readers *need* this bibliotherapy, one way or another. No wonder the genre has a well-entrenched tradition of delegitimizing its own agenda. But in an ironic twist, in being unable to avoid the duality of repression and liberation, queer YA novels do consistently normalize queer sexuality in at least one way. Foucault claims that our culture is unable to separate sexuality from discourses of pain and pleasure. In that sense, then, *Dance on My Grave, Baby Be-Bop, Deliver Us from Evie,* and *Good Moon Rising* do in some way affirm queer sexuality, for these books depict it in the discursive mixture of pleasure and pain typical of any description of human sexuality.

As Kirk Fuoss points out, "Because YA texts dealing with homosexuality are embedded in a complex network of power relations, no single agent of power is exclusively responsible for the deployment of strategies" that YA authors use in developing the genre (171). But the discourse in these novels does determine the issues of power surrounding homosexuality; discourse all too often *is* power here: "Discourse transmits and produces power; it reinforces it, but also undermines and exposes it, renders it fragile and makes it possible to thwart it" (Foucault, *History* 101). It is not so much the affirmation of homosexuality or lesbianism, or even the incipient delegitimization, that matters in these novels. Rather, it is the fluid discourse between these two poles, the way knowledge of homosexuality or lesbianism produces both pain and pleasure, that needs investigation; it is the power of discourse to determine these characters' sense of sexuality and even sense of self that is most likely to affect the adolescent reader.

All of the characters who are exploring their sexuality in these novels do so discursively. That is, the conversations and the word choices they use to define their orientation matter far more than their actions do. Sex, after all, is largely interstitial in these novels. But sexuality, that is another matter. Hal self-consciously uses discourse to explore his feelings for his lover in *Dance on My Grave*. He recognizes himself as discursively formed when he says that writing his story is what has changed him, not living his life. *Baby Be-Bop* has a similar self-consciousness about language: the genie specifically instructs Dirk to tell his story, to be the teller of his own story, for it is in the restorying process that power is restored to the marginalized. Evie and her lover Patsy reject their parents' attempts to discursively regulate them by living in an environment that allows them freedom from repression in *Deliver Us from Evie*. And the focus of Jan and Kerry's self-identification as lesbians is not their lovemaking, it is their public proclamation of the fact that they are queer. Words matter far more than actions in their eventual self-affirmation. Given that literary characters are always already and only discursive constructs, the discursive nature of lesbianism and homosexuality in these novels may be unavoidable. But it is important to note that these novels parallel Foucault's flawed conception of sexuality as primarily discursive. Denying the corporeality of homosexuality too easily divorces it from pleasure, which potentially disempowers gay sexuality.

In any event, all four of these YA novels rely on discourse as a

form of power; the two more overtly influenced by postmodernism — *Dance on My Grave* and *Baby Be-Bop* — directly communicate to the reader that power is defined by discourse. These
books all assume at some level a premise central to AIDS awareness: silence equals death. Words equal empowerment. As a genre,
then, queer YA literature necessitates the study of discourse because it is frequently predicated on the foundation that human
sexuality is determined by discourse and that discourse is power.
Foucault's work is most useful to us in the study of queer YA literature if we use his theories to understand the ways in which the
discourse of sexuality in Western tradition has influenced the depiction of gay sexuality. Even if the genre has developed a sense
of self-awareness, its largely negative rhetoric still denies the validation one might wish to find in YA novels about being gay.

YA novels about queer characters often expose sexuality as a
discursive concept, as an act that is regulated more by language
than by any biological factor. But whether YA novels involve
straight characters, gay characters, or both, sexuality serves as a
prominent site of power for the adolescents in these books, precisely because it is regulated by language. Adolescents use their
sexuality to attract other people, to dominate other people, to submit to other people, to enjoy other people, to manipulate other
people, to communicate with other people — in short, sexuality
is a way for them to engage the Other. Discovering their sexuality is powerful to adolescents because it represents a new forum
in which to interact with the Other. *Jouissance*, especially, brings
with it at least the temporary illusion of unifying the Self and the
Other, of an Imaginary healing of the division created by the subject's entrance into the Symbolic Order. The division of the Self
from the Other necessitated by language at once creates the inevitability of sexuality as a discursive construct and brings with it the
power (and pleasure) of knowing the Other. Perhaps this is why
experiencing sex serves as a rite of passage for so many teenagers.
The experience of sexuality may indeed mark a new level of discursive consciousness for adolescents struggling to understand
the distinction between themselves and the Others who constitute
the society in which they must live.

Sometimes, teenage characters in adolescent literature are em-

powered by their newfound knowledge of and pleasure in nego-
tiating with the Other by using sexuality as the currency of interaction, but more often adolescents are disempowered by the
consequences of their sexual actions. In other words, sexuality is
a source of power and pleasure for many adolescents in YA novels,
yet more novelists are comfortable portraying sexuality in terms
of displeasure than pleasure. The novelists who do so seem to be
reinforcing the dynamic of authority within adolescent literature
that reminds adolescents of their place within the power structure.
Sex may be one of the first times they become aware of their own
power — but negative depictions of human sexuality provide the
author with an occasion to remind the adolescent not to become
too powerful, not to become too enamored with their knowledge
of pleasure. Because adults are quite conscious of sexuality as a
source of power, they frequently subject adolescent readers to
very consistent ideologies that attempt to regulate teen sexuality
by repressing it. Much of the discourse that creates human sexuality is designed to do exactly that: discourse creates and subsequently regulates sexuality as it does all forms of human power.

CHAPTER 5

# *"When I can control the focus"*

DEATH AND NARRATIVE RESOLUTION

IN ADOLESCENT LITERATURE

## *Death in the Young Adult Novel*

In Chapter 4, I discussed Foucault's concept of sexuality as a human construct invented to control the biological aspects of sex (*History* 35). Death is another biological imperative. It is, perhaps, even more powerful in the human mind than sexuality, for although in theory some individuals can live asexually, no one avoids death. Moreover, humans have created numerous institutions surrounding the biological reality of death to help them control its power: most religions, for example, have institutional investments in explaining death to people. For many adolescents, trying to understand death is as much of a rite of passage as experiencing sexuality is.

The standard interpretation of *The Catcher in the Rye* provides a noteworthy example: Playing the antiestablishment antihero in a picaresque set in New York, Holden wears a red hat to invoke his dead brother's memory; Allie, who has died of leukemia, was a redhead. Holden wants to be a catcher in the rye because he wants to keep children like his classmate James Castle, who has jumped to his death from a dormitory window, from falling into death. Holden does not begin to heal spiritually until he watches his little sister riding a merry-go-round (symbolic, perhaps, of the life cycle) and recognizes that he has to let her take chances, including the chance that she might die. He cannot catch her — or anyone — to prevent her death.

Two of the first *Entwicklungsromane* directly marketed to young adults in the 1960s are similarly focused on death: Ponyboy in *The Outsiders* and John and Lorraine in *The Pigman* work through their grief about a friend's death by writing their stories. Children's and adolescent novels including *Bridge to Terabithia* (1977) and *Toning the*

*Sweep* demonstrate characters working through the five stages of grief that Elisabeth Kübler-Ross identifies: denial, anger, guilt, depression, acceptance. Death and grief are, indeed, common topics in this literature.

The greatest difference between how death is portrayed in children's and adolescent literature, however, lies perhaps in the use to which death is put in the literary text. According to Karen Coats, children's literature is very much defined by children learning to separate from their parents ("Lacan with Runt Pigs" 116–120). Books from *The Runaway Bunny* to *Harriet the Spy* demonstrate children learning to individuate by separating from their actual or symbolic parents. Many children's books are about death: *Charlotte's Web* and *Tuck Everlasting* are two important examples. But in both of these books (and in many children's books about death), death is portrayed as part of a cycle, as an ongoing process of life. Learning about death seems to be a stage in the child's process of separating from the parent more than anything else. Wilbur, for example, becomes an adult only after death separates him from his mother figure, Charlotte; Winnie Foster in *Tuck Everlasting* matures most in the incident in which she chooses to separate from her actual parents. Although her friends the Tucks will never die, she herself chooses death, in a symbolic separation from her mother figure, Mae Tuck, when she refuses to drink the water that could make her immortal.

Mortality, however, has a different purpose in adolescent literature. In this genre, protagonists come to understand that death is more than a symbolic separation from the parent. Acknowledging death is more than a stage necessary toward growing up and away from one's parents. Death in adolescent literature is a threat, an experience adolescents understand as a finality. Few adolescent novels use the cycle imagery that dominates books like *Tuck Everlasting* and *Charlotte's Web* because the *Bildungsroman* formula mandates a plot determined by the concept of growth as linear: death is the endpoint of that line. Adolescent literature thus sustains narrative investigations into death that are more than symbolic journeys into separation from the parent. Indeed, I would submit that death is the sine qua non of adolescent literature, the defining factor that distinguishes it both from children's and adult literature. In children's literature, learning about death symbolizes a degree of separation from one's parents; adult literature confronts death from such a variety of intricate perspectives that it seems difficult to trace a pattern on the topic. But in adolescent literature, death is often depicted in terms of maturation when the protagonist accepts the permanence of mortality, when s/he accepts herself as Being-towards-death.[1] *Little Women* provides an example: in the first half of the novel, Jo fears death and learns a healthy respect for it, but in the second half, Jo's life experiences are determined by the death of her sister. She makes the decisions she makes about her work and her love life because of the permanent rupture in her life caused by her sister's death. Beth's death is important not only for how it causes Jo to acknowledge her separateness from her sister. Certainly, Beth's death does lead Jo to that recognition. But Beth's death also influences Jo's maturation. She returns to her family; she writes in a different voice; and she marries a man inconceivable to her in the first book of the text. Jo learns about death, but even more, she works through her grief and discovers a way to accommodate her grief by living her life in ways that acknowledge both her pain at losing a loved one and her awareness of her own mortality.

Acceptance of losing others and awareness of mortality shape much of the discourse surrounding death in YA novels. Both acceptance and awareness serve in the power/knowledge dynamic to render the adolescent both powerless in her fear of death and empowered by acknowledging its power. Adolescents often gain their first knowledge of the pain permanent separation involves when they feel powerless because someone they love dies; the corollary that inevitably follows is adolescents' recognition of their own mortality. If my brother Allie is dead, then I, Holden, will also be dead some day. In the calm that follows the emotional storm, adolescent characters usually seem more empowered than they did when they still denied death's power, as Holden Caulfield's narrative demonstrates. It seems that death has far more power over the adolescent imagination than any human institution possibly could. Thus, I will first discuss how the resulting acceptance and awareness of this power leads to at least three recurring patterns surrounding the depiction of death in YA novels. Then I will examine how death is tied to issues of subjectivity and objectivity by exploring how authors of YA novels including Lois

Lowry, Francesca Lia Block, and Trudy Krisher use photography to explore Being-towards-death. Finally, I will investigate how Being-towards-death is implicated in narrative structure in these novels in a complex fusion of theme and structure.

## DEATH OCCURS ONSTAGE

In many children's novels, characters such as Charlotte die off-stage, and their death is reported by indirect narration or in the speech of another character. Death in the YA novel is far more immediate. When Johnny kills a Soc, Bob, in *The Outsiders*, the text describes Bob's corpse unflinchingly. Later, Ponyboy describes watching Johnny die. The reader is not protected from either death by the filter of indirect narration. Jamal watches his friend Tito shoot a gang member during a robbery in *Scorpions*. Adam Farmer witnesses his parents' death in *I Am the Cheese*. In Karen Hesse's *Out of the Dust* (1997), Billie Joe tells the reader directly, "Ma died that day / giving birth to my brother" (69). She describes her mother's funeral, too, in language that does not flinch from death: "They wrapped my baby brother in a blanket / and placed him in Ma's bandaged arms. / We buried them together" (70). This confrontation with death seems essential for adolescents to gain knowledge of death's power and of their own powerlessness over it.

## DEATH IS UNTIMELY, VIOLENT, AND UNNECESSARY

Part of what seems to force many adolescent characters into their recognition of death's power is the seemingly gratuitous nature of some deaths. More children's novels deal with the elderly dying than with children or teenagers dying, but in YA novels, adolescents learn about their own mortality by witnessing the death of someone who is not necessarily going gently into that good night. Myers's *Scorpions* illustrates this phenomenon with its graphic message about the results of gang activity. In that novel Jamal's friend Tito kills another teenager to protect Jamal's life. Jamal learns from watching Tito's pain that life is hard and cold (215–216). In *Toning the Sweep*, Emily learns that her grandfather was lynched as a young man while she reconciles herself to her grandmother's premature death from cancer. In *Lyddie*, the protagonist's mother and sister die deaths that result, at least in part, from inadequate medical attention. All of Mollie Hunter's *A Sound of Chariots* (1972) and much of the *Bildungsroman* that Betty Smith wrote, *A Tree Grows in Brooklyn* (1943), are testimonies to the narrators' grief for their prematurely dead fathers. In the former, Bridie's father dies from complications with his war wounds; in the latter, Francie's father dies from alcoholism-induced complications. Cynthia Voigt's *David and Jonathan* (1992) deals with Holocaust grief — as do almost all books about the Holocaust, except Lois Lowry's *Number the Stars* (1989). Lowry's *The Giver* (1993) is far more convincing as a Holocaust novel because it contains a compelling image of genocide when a baby is killed for not fitting into his culture. In fact, Anne Frank's *Diary* (1952) is often the most effective book I teach because students are deeply affected by the death of a historical person at the age of fifteen. Students new to the narrative of death's power who have been trained as readers in a culture immersed in the avoidance of death assume that Anne will live and are often shocked that she does not.

TRAGIC LOSS OF INNOCENCE

Understanding Being-towards-death leads adolescent characters into a loss of innocence that seems, at least initially, tragic. Wilbur is scared of dying, but he does not seem headed for self-destruction because of his knowledge of death. Holden Caulfield does. Ged, in Le Guin's *A Wizard of Earthsea*, looses catastrophe on his world when he releases his own death from the underworld. Only in confronting his own mortality, naming it, and accepting it can Ged obliterate the destructive incubus that he, in his prideful innocence, has inflicted on himself and Earthsea. Laura transforms herself into a witch in Mahy's *The Changeover* (1984) to defeat the incubus that is killing her brother. Her transformation is permanent, as is her power over the incubus she eventually kills. Holden, Ged, and Laura grow only because they recognize and accept themselves as Being-towards-death. Before they come to this stage of acceptance, they seem poised for an inevitable fall created by their own vulnerability. When they overcome their tragic vulnerability and avert catastrophe, transforming the tragedy of their own mortality into at least some level of triumph, they experience a heightened awareness of what power they do and do not hold in their lives.

## Death and Dominant Discourse

It is not without significance that the discourse surrounding death recurs in adolescent literature with the consistency of the two other dominant discourses of the YA novel, the establishment of an identity independent from one's parents and the exploration of sexuality. Death, authority, and sexuality are mutually implicated. Adolescents understand that their biological parents had sex to conceive them. What they may not always acknowledge—although the fact is indisputable — is that sex exists as a biological antidote to death. Species procreate because they are mortal. Judeo-Christian tradition links sex and death in its master narrative that sex did not exist until Adam and Eve became mortal and were expelled from the Garden of Eden. I have always suspected that authority figures in our culture protect children from knowledge of sex because of our cultural desire to protect children from a knowledge of death. Philippe Ariès refers to this as the "interdict laid upon death" in the twentieth century (2). The romantic image of the innocent child still dominating our culture perpetuates the illusion that children flourish best if they are free from the corrupting knowledge of carnality. Carnality: sex and death, death and sex. They are cultural and biological concepts that are linked inviolably.

Aidan Chambers's *Breaktime* illustrates how sex and death are linked discursively in adolescent literature. In Chapter 4, I used *Breaktime* as an example of a novel in which sex serves as a rite of passage for the protagonist, Ditto. The novel depicts a boy who gains empathy for his father once he has had sex. Ditto's father eventually tells him, "Maybe we should both try harder to see each other's point of view" (172). But one significant narrative fact remains: Ditto needs to gain empathy for his father because the boy fears that his father, who has suffered a heart attack during a fight with Ditto, is dying. While his father is in the hospital and Ditto is en route to an assignation with his lover, Helen, he witnesses one of his mates fight with his own father. Ditto's recognition that they lack empathy for one another is central to his ability to develop empathy for his own father — as is the revelation that Ditto's father gave up his dreams of riding motocross when he was eighteen. In other words, Ditto's losing his virginity is not the sole prerequisite of Ditto's gained empathy, but death and sex are clearly linked. In one comic scene, for example, Ditto describes an undertaker's daughter forcing her sexual attentions on one of his friends. They have intercourse in a coffin (130–131).

In fact, the text eventually establishes Ditto as an unreliable narrator who may have invented having intercourse with Helen as a story he has spun for a school chum. (The fact of his father's heart attack and Ditto's gained empathy for him are indisputably established, however.) Ditto's school chum has challenged him that "literature is, by definition, a lie" (6). Ditto then uses discourse to tell the tale of his father's heart attack, the fight he has witnessed between a mate and his father, and intercourse with Helen to dispute the claim that fiction is not truthful. Ditto refuses to identify which portions of his narrative have "really" happened, but the fact that he links sex and death in his own discursive creation indicates their apposition in his mind. Thus, Ditto relies on discourse to create a narrative about power, authority, sex, and death. That he employs these factors to define his own growth indicates the interrelationship of these issues in adolescent literature.

## Death, Photography, and Language

But Young Adult novels complicate death as a literary topic not only in the thematic subject of death as a matter of content, but also by incorporating it in subtle ways into the very narrative structure of the novel itself. The relationship between death as subject and death informing narrative structure becomes especially apparent in YA novels about photography, for photography affords YA novelists an opportunity to explore the relationship between agency, death, and discourse. That is, as adolescents come to understand themselves as agents, as acting subjects, they can also begin to understand better the relationship between life and death. Novels that employ photography create many opportunities for characters to explore metaphorically the relationship between subject and object, between acting and being acted upon. This dichotomy between agency and passivity that is embedded in language as the relationship between subject and object creates narrative instances of Being-towards-death so that the narrative itself becomes implicated in the exploration of what it means to die. To demonstrate how YA novels can comment on death both thematically and structurally, I will first discuss photography theory and demonstrate how it has bearing on issues of subjectivity and objectivity in three YA novels: Lois Lowry's *A Summer to Die* (1977), Francesca Lia Block's *Witch Baby* (1991), and Trudy Krisher's *Spite Fences* (1994); then I will analyze how death and narrative structure are linked in these novels.

All of these novels employ photographing protagonists as metaphors for the relationship between power and agency. The metaphor of the camera bestowing upon the photographer a sense of empowerment based on the communicative abilities of photographs occurs often in literature.[2] *A Summer to Die*, *Witch Baby*, and *Spite Fences* demonstrate the protagonist employing photography as a metaphorical representation for achieving agency. The intricacy of the photography metaphor also allows these narratives to explore the nature of subjectivity as constructed by language while simultaneously foregrounding Being-towards-death as an issue of both theme and narrative structure. In other words, the relationship between the protagonist's increased awareness of the subject-object relationship occurs in conjunction with her maturing into some sort of acceptance of the grief that accompanies death and loss. Moreover, the parallel lines of the character's understanding of subjectivity and of death pass through a series of points created by the repetition of various photographs. Viewing these pictures from differing vantage points increases each character's perspicacity. The protagonist must experience this series of photographic repetitions in order to achieve resolution in both the photographic and the narrative sense: she must perceive herself clearly in order to achieve the emotional resolution that seems at times almost de rigueur in adolescent literature.[3] Thus, photography affects both content and form in *A Summer to Die*, *Witch Baby*, and *Spite Fences*.

In *Camera Lucida*, an extended essay on photography, Roland Barthes discusses how the fluid relationship between subject and object becomes an issue in the art of photography when a camera negotiates the space between them.[4] The photographer has agency and the photograph itself does not, for it is an artifact, but the camera is an object that transforms images of people — acting subjects — into objects, in the process giving them a new significance they might not have previously held. As Martha Banta notes, the concept of "camera vision" reflects the tendency of the wandering human eye to focus on one object; the act of focusing singles out the object, giving it importance (26). Indeed, the earliest portrait photos "transformed subject into object, and even one might say, into a museum object: in order to take the first portraits (around 1840) the subject had to assume long poses under a glass roof in bright sunlight; to become an object made one suffer as much as a surgical operation" (Barthes 13). The camera and the act of photography demonstrate that the relationship between subject and object is often continuous rather than discrete; separating the actor from the acted upon is not always easy. As Marianne Hirsch puts it, "we both look and are looked at . . . the subject is installed in the social through that double, mutual, perceptual relationship which makes every spectator also a spectacle" (103). In a photograph, "the looking subject is always already *in* the image, shaping it with his or her own reflection or projection" (Hirsch 103, emphasis in the original). The photograph is therefore a unique artifact in the way that it is capable of capturing at once images of the individual's subjectivity and objectivity. In this dual role, then, photography shares one similarity with language: both depend on the subject-object relationship and the fluid relationship between them to function. Photography bears another relationship to language in the way that it forces us to consider the relationship between signifier and signified. Whereas Saussure has taught us to separate the signifier from the signified in linguistic constructions, Barthes points out that photographs are a type of signifier immediately indistinguishable from the signified.[5] Is the picture itself a signifier, representing some other object, or is it signified, itself an artifact communicating directly to the viewer?[6]

It is perhaps for this reason — because of the unique way that cameras allow adolescents to blend subject and object, to integrate signifier and signified — that adolescent novels employ camera metaphors as a way to explore agency as a linguistic construct that empowers the adolescent. The three novels I am discussing also provide characters with some of the tendencies Susan Sontag identifies for photography: in their ubiquity and passivity, photographs can become a source of aggression (7), and cameras can create a sense of vicariousness (10) that may also sanction the photographer's nonintervention in painful issues (11). For characters who take pictures instead of becoming involved, photography can become a source of complicity, a way to approve tacitly that which they might not otherwise be able to change (12). Cameras serve to both empower and disempower adolescents' agency. What holds true for Sontag holds true in each of these three novels: the photographic act and the character's capacity to view the photograph matter more than the photograph itself. Not surprisingly, given the didactic ideological impulse that shapes so much adolescent fiction, most adolescent novels that employ photographic metaphors value the function of taking pictures over the form of the final product. Pictures are important not so much in and of themselves but for what they teach the adolescent, especially as they become repeated artifacts that allow the character to witness the same scene during several different points in her or his development.[7] As a result, the process of photography engages the fictional adolescent's agency in a way that enables the character to embrace her or his subjectivity.

## A Summer to Die

Lois Lowry's *A Summer to Die* is a clear-cut example of this tendency. Most of the story is about Meg's reactions to her sister Molly as Molly dies of leukemia. Meg's camera is crucial to her acceptance of Molly's death; before she realizes that her sister has a fatal disease, Meg cares more about her camera than almost anything (9, 67). She says, "All those times when I feel awkward and inept — all those times are made up for when I have my camera, when I can look through the viewfinder and feel that I can control the focus and the light and the composition, when I can capture what I see, in a way that no one else is seeing it" (29). These final clauses identify Meg's photography as a crucial aspect of her exploration of subjectivity and objectivity: she wants to claim for herself what she sees, to own it, hold it captive, as she would any object; but most important, she wants to prove that her perceptions are different from everyone else's. She explores her subjectivity by manipulating photographic objects. Meg's insistence on manipulating the subject and object sets up the text's awareness that language is predicated on perceptions of subjectivity and objectivity. Meg's experiments seem like metaphorical experiments with language as well, especially in the way that Meg is concerned with how the pictures she takes communicate something to other people.

Meg even recognizes that her imagistic interpretations of those she has photographed must have an effect on their sense of their own subjectivity: "It must be a funny feeling, I think, to see your own face like that, caught by someone else, with all your feelings showing in it" (48). As Barthes says, "In front of the lens, I am . . . the one I think I am, the one I want others to think I am, the one the photographer thinks I am, and the one he makes use of to exhibit his art" (13). In identifying four positions on a continuum from subject to object position that the photographed person holds, Barthes outlines the nuances a photograph can contain. Meg intuitively understands them when she says, "I care about the expressions on people's faces, the way the light falls onto them, and the way the shadows are in soft patterns and contrast" (113). She cares most about the two object positions that Barthes identifies: how she perceives people and how she can transform their images into art. To Meg, her art is a matter of engaging her agency to transform other people into objects *as a way to communicate to them.* Her camera is her language; the resulting pictures are her specific speech acts.[8]

Meg acknowledges consciously the importance of processing her pictures herself. She recognizes how to use processing as a way to "compensate for all sorts of things, how to build up contrast, how to reduce it" (80). It is the process of achieving a final product that has the resolution of her choosing, not necessarily the end product itself, that empowers Meg. In other words, Meg recognizes that the photographic process entails more than just *granting* agency to the person taking the picture; agency can be *achieved* in the photographic process, as agency can also be achieved within the process of constructing ourselves of language. As Catharine Belsey notes, the subject is constructed by language and by the exterior forces that language asserts upon the individual (Belsey 46–50), for — as Lacan puts it — the unconscious mind is itself constructed like a language system (*Four* 149).[9] In this sense, Meg's photographic equipment also serves as a metaphor for the unconscious mind: within the equipment lies the structures necessary to discern and to blend the differences between subject and object.

Despite the intricacy with which Lowry imbues Meg's use of photography, the greatest flaw in this book is how easy the camera makes birth and death experiences for Meg. In that, the book fulfills Sontag's definition of photographer as voyeur and nonparticipant. In this case, the voyeurism deprives Meg of agency and, therefore, of some degree of maturity. For example, a friend of Meg's delivers a baby as quickly and painlessly as a character in a soap opera. Meg has been asked to photograph the birth, and she deals with her panic in this situation by hiding behind her camera: "I lifted my camera and photographed Maria smiling. The instant I had the camera in my hands, things felt comfortable. The light was good; the settings fell into place as I manipulated them; everything was okay" (128). Meg and the reader are both deprived of any sense of the necessary pain surrounding childbirth. Moreover, Meg's sister Molly dies offstage so that Meg does not have to witness the pain of death firsthand, either. Apparently, although her parents think that she is old enough to watch someone being born, she is not old enough to watch someone die.

Significantly, however, Meg reconciles herself to her grief over Molly's death by gazing at a photograph of herself taken by a friend.

> It was a large photograph, against a white mount, framed in a narrow black frame, and it was not just the coincidence of a stranger who happened to look like me; it was my face. It was taken at an angle; the wind was blowing my hair, and I was looking off in the distance somewhere, far beyond the meticulously trimmed edges of the photograph or the rigid confines of its frame. The outline of my neck and chin and half-turned cheek was sharp against the blurred and subtle shapes of pine trees in the background. . . . There was something of Molly in my face. It startled me, seeing it. The line that defined my face, the line that separated the darkness of the trees from the light that curved into my forehead and cheek was the same line that

had once identified Molly by its shape. The way I held my shoulders was the way she had held hers. It was a transient thing, I knew, but when Will had held the camera and released the shutter for one five-hundredth of a second, he had captured it and made permanent whatever of Molly was in me. I was grateful, and glad. (150–151)

The emotional climax of the book occurs when Meg for the first time views herself as an object in a photograph. As John Stephens notes, Meg "breaks into a new way of seeing and a new subject position" from this experience (286). Meg has now experienced the subject position — that is, a position of action, of agency— and the object position.

This need to recognize one's own agency is a central pattern of adolescent literature; we achieve adulthood more comfortably if we recognize that we have some control over the various subject positions we occupy than if we feel entirely like objects, pawns, in other people's movements. But conversely, maturity also depends on our ability to maintain, when necessary, an object position, for we are all objects of the cultural forces that constantly shape us. Again, the relationship between subject and object is a fluid one, but gaining an increased understanding of one's power as an acting subject is inevitable during maturation. Sontag focuses on the cultural power photography gives the photographing subject: "To photograph is to appropriate the thing photographed. It means putting oneself into a certain relation to the world that feels like knowledge — and, therefore, power" (4). For Meg, the power of knowledge occurs from taking and seeing photographs. She only achieves the pleasure of knowledge/power when she has experienced both the subject and the object positions afforded by photography, after she has been both photographing subject and photographed object.

## Witch Baby

Francesca Lia Block's *Witch Baby* also ties issues of subjectivity and objectivity to issues of maturity by means of photography metaphors. A postmodern fairy tale like its predecessor *Weetzie*

*Bat, Witch Baby* is the story of the eponymous character who asks, "What time are we upon and where do I belong?" (3, 9, 15). Suffering from the same sense of fragmentation that Sharon Wilson identifies as common in Margaret Atwood's novels dealing with photography (31), Witch Baby understands neither her paternity nor her culture, postmodern Los Angeles. As she seeks to better understand them both, she grows to recognize her subjectivity. Witch Baby is confused about her identity because her parents have not been honest with her. She was abandoned as an infant at the home of Weetzie Bat and her significant other, whose name is My Secret Agent Lover Man; Weetzie and My Secret have not told her that he is her biological father. Much of Witch Baby's identity is defined by her jealousy for Weetzie's biological daughter, Cherokee. Witch Baby has dark, tangled hair and slanting purple eyes; she is mysterious and very angry.

When it comes to photography, Witch Baby is like Meg in that she takes pictures from the outset of the narrative, but she is never the object of any photo. "Witch Baby had taken photographs of everyone in her almost-family. . . . Because she had taken all the pictures herself, there was no witch child with dark tangled hair and tilted purple eyes" in her collection of pictures pasted on the family clock (3). She sees but feels herself to be unseen; she lives in the shadow of her vibrant sister, Cherokee.

When a boy Witch Baby has a crush on hears her play the drums, she is pleased by his attention: "It was as if she were being seen by someone for the first time" (23). But she grieves because My Secret Agent Lover Man does not recognize how similar the two of them are in both worrying about the pain in the world around them; both of them recognize themselves as Being-towards-death. Witch Baby even tapes three articles or news photos to her wall each night that detail something wrong with the world; one of these articles about a group of Native Americans who have died of radiation poisoning inspires My Secret Agent Lover Man to make a movie. Later, Witch Baby is again pleased when another friend, Coyote, sees how similar she is to him and to My Secret Agent Lover Man in that they share a mutual grief about world issues. She thinks of Coyote, "But he recognizes that I am like him and My Secret doesn't see" (31). Feeling that the (Name-of-the-)Father cannot see her causes Witch Baby even more pain.

Throughout the story, Witch Baby continues to snap pictures of her family and their life together, of homeless people on the street, of people dying of AIDS, of the beach, of the redwood forest. She continues to ask herself and other people where she belongs. Eventually, she learns that My Secret Agent Lover Man is her father. She runs away to seek her biological mother, Vixanne Wigg, and is disillusioned when she discovers that Vixanne is the leader of a Jayne Mansfield cult that does nothing but watch Mansfield movies, eat sugar, and deny that evil exists in the world. Trying to communicate that these attempts to escape from pain are futile, Witch Baby leaves behind her a series of photographs that she has taken of homeless people and victims of AIDS; she hopes her mother "will look at them and see" (93). At this juncture in the novel, Witch Baby clearly perceives her photography as a form of language, for these pictures are signifiers of both world angst and Witch Baby's feelings. Only through photographs can she communicate to Vixanne what she cares most about.

Witch Baby finally returns home, where her father recognizes how much alike they are and where the other members of her family also voice their appreciation of her. The family's final tribute to Witch Baby is to pose for a family portrait, but this time with the camera on a timer so that Witch Baby can be included in the picture. Witch Baby looks around at the people in this family portrait and recognizes their pain and their grief: some fear AIDS, others have lost their beloved; some suffer from discrimination, others mourn "for the sky and sea, animals and vegetables, that were full of toxins" (102). Yet she finally understands that "her own sadness was only a small piece of the puzzle of pain that made up the globe. But she was a part of the globe — she had her place" (102–103). Witch Baby has gained a sense of identity, but she cannot fully claim the subject position until she recognizes that the people around her accept her in both the object and the subject position. Her transformation seems to be much like Meg's in *A Summer to Die*: Witch Baby needs to understand herself as object before she can place herself within the matrix of her own subject positions. The process of photography leads Witch

Baby and Meg to their transcendent understanding of their own agency.

## Spite Fences

*Spite Fences*, by Trudy Krisher, employs photography metaphors in a narrative that explores racial tension. Thirteen-year-old Maggie Pugh uses her camera as a way to look at life in small-town Georgia in 1960. Throughout the narrative, when she wants to evaluate a situation, she thinks of it in terms of a freeze-frame, telling herself, *"Aim. Click. . . . Advance the film. Trip the shutter. . . . Focus. Click"* (2). Maggie, who is white, receives the camera as a gift from a black friend named Zeke after she starts teaching him to read because she thinks he does not know how to read the word *white* on a rest room door. Because he has used the rest room, he is arrested and beaten, and later brutalized by a mob that urinates on him and masturbates over his unconscious body. Maggie, hidden from the mob in a tree, has witnessed the near-lynching of her friend. Her fear for her friend's life causes her to recognize herself as Being-towards-death. Never before has she confronted mortality. Ultimately, she agrees to serve as a witness in court so that his case can be prosecuted. She wants to quit living in fear of other people's violence. Her words thus have the power to change the course of her hometown's history.

Maggie learns to respect the Civil Rights movement that is unfolding around her, but she must also learn how to handle the effects of institutionalized racism on white people, specifically on her mother and on their spiteful neighbors. Maggie's mother beats her after seeing photographs of Maggie with some of her black friends. The next-door neighbor has already tried to rape her. In an ugly altercation between the two families, Maggie's camera gets broken, and she is devastated. She recognizes that because of the evil of racism "everything" in her hometown is as "smashed and broken to bits" as her camera is by the effects of racism (171). But when her best girlfriend gives her a new single-lens camera, she says she feels, "for the first time in my whole life, like I'd finally been *born*" (195).

For Maggie, the perspective the camera provides her is more

than a matter of feeling a sense of agency — it is a matter of expressing truth. Thus, as the text unravels, Maggie identifies occupying the subject position as seeing and speaking the truth. Early in the text, Zeke has told her, "Never be afraid of the truth" (12). When he gives Maggie her first camera, he tells her, "I got you this camera, Maggie, to help you with the truth. So you'll first trust your eyes to see it and then trust your own voice to tell it" (102). In order for Maggie to quit being a victim of racism, classism, physical abuse, and sexual assault, she needs to learn to be honest and to be vocal. And she uses photography as her voice to express the truth as she sees it. She even demonstrates how language and photography are related for her when she describes her memories of Zeke's brutalization: "They were images inside me that I wanted to forget, but they were things, in truth, that I needed to remember. They were the undeveloped pictures in the camera of my mind" (182).

When the African-American people of Maggie's community stage a sit-down at a lunch counter that white supremacists turn into a riot, Maggie takes pictures that capture the horror of the violence. She tells herself, *"Trip the shutter, Maggie. You know what you're seeing here. You've got to get it down"* (271). The rioters assault one of her closest friends, and she says, "What filled my lens was more than the blood gushing from my sweet friend. It was the red color of the fence, the red color of the earth on which I stood. It was red, the color of my life this summer. . . . Red: it was the color of [my hometown]" (272). The photographs Maggie takes that day win a contest and are published in *Life* magazine as part of a series on racial violence during the Civil Rights movement. Maggie's mother cannot forgive her for befriending people of another race, so at the text's end, Maggie and her mother are estranged. Maggie accepts the necessity of their emotional distance, however, for she recognizes that her mother will never respect her daughter's agency. But because Maggie has found a life's work that foregrounds her subjectivity in ways that she values, and because she has found friends who respect that subjectivity, Maggie has grown into a self-acceptance that indicates her maturity.

Maggie, like Meg and Witch Baby, has used photography as a physical expression of the primacy of her interiority. Operating the camera represents her internal process of claiming the subject position. More than any of these other novels, *Spite Fences* openly expresses the result of photography as a matter of expressing truth. But the photographs all of these characters take ultimately represent truth for each of them. And a central truth that each of these novels shares is the implication that without the camera — that is, without her individual artistic representation of language and, it therefore follows, without some form of language itself — the character would remain powerless, a victim stranded in the object position of some other camera's gaze.

## Death and Photography

Significantly, these novels also share the concern with death that is so common in adolescent literature. *A Summer to Die* identifies the topic in the title; Meg experiences and eventually reconciles herself to her sister's death. Witch Baby's anxieties can almost all be traced back to a strong sense of grief for the death of living things: she fears the destruction of the environment and what the AIDS pandemic does to people; she fears serial killers and what will happen to the missing children pictured on milk cartons; she fears "nuclear accidents, violence, poverty and disease" (8), and she mourns for "families dying of radiation, old people in rest homes listening for sirens, ragged men and women wandering barefoot through the city, becoming ghosts because no one wanted to see them" (92). Maggie experiences the metaphorical death of her relationship with her mother, but even more important, she experiences the near-death of her friend Zeke who is almost lynched. Her fear of the violence her friend has suffered creates in her a new fear that seems to be linked to the fear of death. Certainly the fear she feels for Zeke's life is the greatest emotional transformation of her life. The experience is a chilling one.

These characters, like so many in adolescent literature, must grapple with Being-towards-death if they are to mature. Acknowledging death occurs as a stage for the protagonist of almost every *Bildungsroman*. Sometimes teenagers such as those in John Knowles's *A Separate Peace* are reckless because they are testing the limits of their mortality; other teenagers — like Elizabeth in Crescent Dragonwagon's *The Year It Rained* (1985) — are obsessively morbid not so much because they are being self-indulgent, but because they are immersing themselves in something they do not understand as a way to try to understand it. Acknowledging death is one mark of maturity; adolescent novels about protagonists who reconcile themselves to grief are clearly targeting this emotional need of adolescents.

Roland Barthes, perhaps, would think it no small coincidence that death permeates these YA novels that are ostensibly about photography. *Camera Lucida* is, after all, his elegy for his mother. Photographs have as their subtext the death of the person photographed; they are both memory and memorial. Barthes has argued not only for the subject-object duality in photography, but also for its conflation of life and death. He calls the photograph "that very subtle moment when, to tell the truth, I am neither subject nor object but a subject who feels he is becoming an object: I then experience a micro-version of death . . . : I am truly becoming a specter" (14).[10] Barthes calls the photographer a type of embalmer (14) and the photograph a "flat Death" (92); the separation between life and death "is reduced to a simple click, the one separating the initial pose from the final print" (92). Every photograph of a person captures in a lifeless position someone who is either dead or will die eventually; in "every photograph is this catastrophe" (Barthes 96). In this, Barthes defines death as the ultimate position of objectivity, for in death the body is completely without agency.

Barthes cites Edgar Morin's observation that the "crisis of death," that is, the beginning of a time when our society became more obsessively negative about death, began in the mid-nineteenth century at about the same time that photography became a cultural institution and about the same time that the *Bildungsroman* emerged as a literary genre (92). It was only shortly after this that developmental psychologists codified adolescence as a stage of life. The very fact that Freud and his followers felt so compelled to compartmentalize the passing stages of our lives marks a cultural view of life as an inexorable march to death. In other words, both photography and developmental psychology confirmed the process of fixing things in time for a culture that was increasingly teleologically oriented.

It seems only natural, then, that people living a stage of their lives that marks them one step closer to a progression toward death would fix on photography as a way of understanding the relationship between life and death. Indeed, adolescence is often the stage of life associated with the individual's first serious grappling with death as an inevitability. Photographs seem to mark a way of slowing the process down for the adolescent characters in these novels. If they can capture truth on film, creating a series of miniature death images for themselves in transforming the subjects around them into objects, perhaps death will not have as much power over them. If they can make time stand still, perhaps they can in some sense defeat death. Even more important, all three of the characters in these novels actually experience the death/object position of the camera's gaze and survive to tell their stories. Indeed, their experiences as objects prove essential to their growth. Photography allows these characters to explore a paradox crucial to their need to understand death: is the camera stopping time or acknowledging its passage? In the illusion of permanence that they afford the photographer, photographs even seem to transcend death, for they can survive long after the photographer and the photographed subject/object are dead.

## Death and Narrative Structure

Basing his argument on Roland Barthes's observation that narrative progression is also an inevitable action, Peter Brooks demonstrates yet another teleological factor at work here ("Freud's Masterplot" 282). Brooks defines the narrative structure of the novel as an avoidance of death. The length of the narrative is designed to circumvent its own death, which is represented by the novel's ending (Brooks, "Freud's Masterplot" 282–283).[11] Narratives avoid their own endings (read: "deaths") specifically by creating a series of repetitions; any series of events allows characters to work toward greater understanding and simultaneously avoid the narrative's own and the reading subject's demise, which will occur when the characters achieve understanding and the narrative ends (Brooks, "Freud's Masterplot" 285–296; Brooks, *Reading for the Plot* 97–109).[12]

In the novels under investigation, photographic images serve strikingly to provide each protagonist with repetitions that move the character closer to the narrative's end and simultaneously delay that movement. For example, Meg in *A Summer to Die* takes a series of pictures of her friend Will (28–29), then views them again when she develops them (45), when she shows them to her mother (46), when she shows them to her sister (49), when she shows them to Will himself (66–67), and when she shows them to her friends Ben and Maria (97). She does not completely understand the implications of her own photography, however, until she sees a different image: herself repeated as an object of Will's photography. Only when the repetition occurs with variation is true resolution in both senses of the term possible: Meg sees herself as a clear, highly resolved image and thus resolves her own crisis by no longer avoiding the implications of her sister's death.

Witch Baby experiences her sense of alienation in a repeated series of family photographs, most notably the pictures she has taken of them and pasted to the face of the clock. The pictures on the clock are described four times in the narrative; that the family's images are affixed to a clock signifies Witch Baby's awareness of the passing of time and of how pictures can transcend that passage (3, 52–53, 82, 100–101). She repeatedly returns to these images until she achieves the variation necessary for resolution by including herself in the final picture, the one she glues at the pinnacle of the clockface over the number twelve (100–101).

For Maggie, the most important repetition is her capturing of the violence waged against peaceful protesters not only when the pictures are developed, but also when they are printed in *Life* magazine. Only when she sees the image replicated in a public forum is she able to assure herself that she has accomplished something meaningful in improving race relations in her hometown. Perhaps her actions have averted other people's needless deaths; in any event, she seems better positioned to accept, as Witch Baby does, the inevitability that much of life is ugly and painful.

For all these characters, then, either one photograph or a series of related photographs provides a recursive way of working through conflict toward resolution.[13] Photographs slow down each narrative's progression toward its own demise, but they also allow each character to resolve her crisis. For Meg, Witch Baby, and Maggie, emotional resolutions involve some sort of acceptance of death. And in each case, photography functions both thematically, implicating the character in related investigations of agency and grief, and structurally, underscoring the impetus of the narrative toward its own death.

Although this tendency is noticeably present in novels about photography, the pattern is also significant in novels that do not necessarily directly link cameras and death, for any number of YA novels have similar recursive moments that slow down the narrative and simultaneously move the plot toward an inexorable conclusion. In Gillian Cross's *Pictures in the Dark* (1996), Charlie Willcox returns several times to photographs of otters. His scrutinizing of the images eventually leads him to understand that his friend Peter is a shape-shifter. During the deathlike trances Peter experiences because of his parents' abuse, he becomes one with the otter. Shape-shifting is his way of escaping his parents' abuse of power. Emily tries to understand an abuse of power so egregious it leads to death in Angela Johnson's *Toning the Sweep*. Her grandfather was lynched by a mob of racist southerners during the Civil Rights movement, and she puts his ghost to rest by videotaping her grandmother and her friends as they talk about the complexities of their lives. For Laura, in Margaret Mahy's *The Changeover*, the repeated image is one an incubus has stamped on her little brother's hand. Every time Laura sees the image, her brother is closer to death. She kills the incubus by stamping her brother's image on its hand; that is, she gains power over the incubus through a variation on the original image. In Aidan Chambers's *Breaktime*, Ditto lusts after a photograph of his girlfriend Helen posing in her bathing suit (20, 22, 39, 51, 52, 72). She is little more than an object to him until he recognizes her sexual agency (76–77). His acknowledgment of it occurs in a conversation filled with self-awareness of discourse, and she then agrees to have sex with him (132–133). After having sex with Helen, no longer able to objectify her, Ditto locks Helen's picture away in a suitcase (177). During the same afternoon, he has made peace with his dying father. The repetition with variation occurs for Ditto when he can no longer view the signified of the photograph as an object. Harry Potter is obsessed with his parents' photographs throughout J. K. Rowling's series. The photograph of his father is particularly influential in helping Harry reconcile himself to his parents' death, especially after the boy enacts what is his father within himself and becomes, temporarily, the image of his own father one magical night (*Prisoner of Azkaban* 212, 407, 427–428). The repeated image in Cormier's *The Chocolate War* that Jerry returns to again and again is less iconic than verbal. A line from "The Love Song of J. Alfred Prufrock" inspires him throughout the text, but he is only able to ask "Do I dare disturb the universe?" because he sees a poster with this line every time he opens his locker. Although Jerry concludes that he has been wrong to try disturbing the universe, Cormier's message to the reader is the opposite: it is Jerry's assailants who have been wrong, it is Jerry's sense of nihilism as he lies dying that is wrong. Cormier wants adolescents to disturb the universe, and he drives his point home by repeating a pivotal phrase so many times in the novel that the reader finally understands its import, even if the protagonist never does. Many YA novels engage similar repetitions. Thematically, these repetitions imply that death is as inevitable as is the eventual ending of each narrative. Thus, death is embedded in the very discourse of much adolescent literature.

Deborah Bowen links death, narrative structure, and photography when she calls photographic imagery "a metaphor for the life-giving and death-dealing enterprise of writing fictions" (22). Photographs paradoxically "offer assurances of identity and clarity; at the same time they undermine the very attempt to control experience by demonstrating that to freeze time and space is to render them obsolete" (Bowen 22). For Barthes, photography is an ontological matter because the "photograph mechanically repeats what could never be repeated existentially" (4). The camera gives these characters the power to transform subject and object. This, in turn, transmutes the effects of death by giving them a tangible means of exploring the linguistic imperatives of sentience as they return as often as necessary to the images that provide them with the opportunity of occupying both the subject and the object position.

In demonstrating how photography serves several functions in adolescent literature, poststructural theory about cameras and photographs provides us with a new way of reading some works of adolescent literature. On the most basic level, novels that include photography demonstrate characters experiencing both subjectivity and objectivity. In that sense, then, photography becomes an extended metaphor for discourse, constructed as it is entirely in terms of the character's (and the reader's) understanding of subjectivity and objectivity. Photographs also serve as a metaphor for death, allowing the adolescents to reconcile themselves to life as a teleological process. In the process of developing this metaphor, photography also serves metonymically in the text by providing a series of stop-action images that serve as the delaying device necessary to the narrative's resolution. The character must experience and reexperience these images in order to achieve the growth that is required of the *Entwicklungsroman* and the *Bildungsroman*. The use of photography in adolescent literature is therefore at once thematic and structural. In employing photography as a metaphor, Lowry, Block, and Krisher demonstrate how inevitably linked agency, discourse, and death are to the actual narrative structure of many novels written for eleven- to fifteen-year-olds.

This combined thematic and structural focus provides the adolescent reader with images of empowered adolescents who better understand agency and the discourses surrounding death. The message to the adolescent reader that people are mortal is clear, but the bleakness of the statement is perhaps mitigated by these texts' confidence in the reader's ability to understand that death is only one of the many phenomena that engage people as subjects and objects. In one sense, however, death is the ultimate and inviolable authority in adolescent literature. Adolescents who come to accept Being-towards-death are teenagers accepting (once again) their own limitations. The discourse of death in adolescent literature therefore represents yet another institutional discourse in which the genre serves to simultaneously empower readers with knowledge and to repress them by teaching them to accept a curtailment of their power. Accepting one's mortality is indeed a powerful rite of passage predicated on understanding oneself as finite. The knowledge of death may thus prove both more repressive and more empowering to adolescents than are discursive interactions with socially constructed institutions, authority figures, or sexuality. Certainly, many novelists for young adults intuitively understand the power and repression that Being-towards-death creates for humans.

That so many narratives written for adolescents systematically depict teenagers engaged in power-repression dynamics indicates to me that the genre carries embedded within it a tacit understanding that adolescents are potentially quite — well — potent. Among other things, adolescents experience these dynamics within institutional discourses that control their understanding of authority and of their physical bodies. If adolescents did not have social and biological power so great that it is defined by authority as needing institutional regulation, the entire genre of the postmodern *Entwicklungsroman* would not have emerged in the form that it has. In the acknowledgment that the very existence of young adult literature authenticates, the genre indeed affirms adolescents' capacity to disturb the universe.

### CHAPTER 6

# Conclusion

## THE POSTSTRUCTURAL PEDAGOGY
## OF ADOLESCENT LITERATURE

The dynamics of power/repression I have discussed in the previous chapters are interrelated. Certainly no institution exists in isolation; no discursive construct possibly can. Since institutions such as school, religion, church, identity politics, and family are invested in socializing adolescents, the depiction of these institutions in adolescent literature are logically implicated in the establishment of narrative authority and in the ideological manipulation of the reader. Cultural representations of death and sex also rely on the adolescent's need to feel empowered and the culture's simultaneous need to repress the adolescent. As a result, discursive representations of adolescents' power and repression can be found integrated in all YA novels.

For example, in Chapter 2 I discussed how M. E. Kerr's novel *Is That You, Miss Blue?* integrates rebellion against school with rebellion against religion. But the novel also shows how rebellion against institutional authority is tied to rebellion against one's parents: Carolyn Cardmaker and Agnes Thatcher found the Atheists Against All Cruelty to punish Carolyn's father (an Episcopalian minister) and the Charles School where they attend boarding school. The pranks these two play allow them to experience a sense of power against their parents, their school, and their church in one fell swoop. Much of the anger the rebels in this book feel resides in their awareness of institutionalized identity politics: Carolyn, Agnes, and the narrator, Flanders, are angry at the Charles School's class-based sorority for reinforcing class stratification. Agnes is angry at the social construction of the deaf in her culture. Flanders is angry with her mother for not maintaining a traditional gender role — an anger that Flanders ultimately resolves when she finally begins talking to her mother again and feels that "I'd been seen and heard on my own" for the first time (158). She expresses her individuation as a discursive construct: she is visually seen as object, she is aurally heard as subject, and so she feels recognized by her mother and thus able to participate in the Symbolic Order.

Sexuality also plays a factor in Flanders's growth. She has an admirer, Sumner Thomas, who conflates sexuality with his fear of mortality. His mother has committed suicide, and Sumner is obsessed with her (70–73, 97, 128–129, 165–166). He explores his obsession discursively, writing poems that Flanders eventually recognizes as a synthesis of his feelings about sex and his feelings about his mother (165). Sumner is re-creating his mother *in logos parentis*, trying to make her manifest in words:

> You are words like "toward," "in," "here," "yes,"
>   "now," "come," and "part of."
> I am sliding.
> You are "hush," "dear," "oh!" "Open," "touch."
> I am sliding.
> You are "darling"
> (I can)
> "always"
> (not)
> "love me"
> (hold)
> "dearest"
> (out)
> "my"
> (much)
> "beloved"
> (longer)
> I am a word like yours. (128–129)

Sumner is Being-towards-death; Flanders recognizes that he must work through his emotional tension with his dead mother before he can grow.

Flanders also watches her teacher Miss Blue lose her sanity. The visual symbol of Miss Blue's martyrdom at the hands of her rebellious students is a portrait of Mary, Queen of Scots, that Miss Blue gazes at desiringly throughout the narrative. Eventually,

Flanders and her friends steal the picture and give it to Miss Blue
to take with her after the Charles School fires her. Since the picture no longer hangs in its shrinelike position in the bathroom,
Flanders experiences the image as one of repetition with variation.
Thereafter, when she thinks of Miss Blue, she thinks of the portrait, feels grief, and fears for her teacher's vulnerability and possible death (169). A recursively used picture that becomes a mark
of Flanders's maturity has resulted from Miss Blue's martyrdom.
Because of Flanders's relationships with Miss Blue and with Sumner, sex, death, and discourse become mutually implicated. No
single event in *Is That You, Miss Blue?* occurs isolated from one
teenage character's perception of the role power and repression
play in her life.

## Pedagogy

In the traditional study of adolescent literature, *Entwicklungsromane* like *Is That You, Miss Blue?* have either been overlooked or
have been studied for their pedagogical value. Caroline Hunt explains why in "Young Adult Literature Evades the Theorists." She
describes the study of Young Adult literature as a field which has
experienced a "striking lack of theoretical criticism" (4) and finds
YA criticism "healthy even if not, or not yet, particularly 'theoretical'" (11). She offers as one reason that the field has developed,
divorced from poststructural critical theory, the fact that many YA
courses are part of teacher certification curricula and so have traditionally been more "applied" than theoretical (8), but she has
encouraged many of us to begin thinking more theoretically: "Today's teachers of YA courses have learned their field, have justified
their existence, and can now go on toward theory if they wish"
(8). One of the underlying agendas of this book has been to demonstrate how important it is that we employ poststructural methodologies when we analyze adolescent literature, since YA novels
are an outgrowth of postmodernism. YA novels depend on the
awareness of the individual as a social being upon which postmodernism insists. Without a postmodern self-consciousness of
individuals as social constructs, the tension between the individual
and institutions that typifies the YA novel would be impossible to

depict. Poststructural theory trains readers to be aware of such postmodern phenomenon. Therefore, by way of conclusion, I hope to identify existing applications of poststructural theory that pertain to the teaching of adolescent literature as a postmodern literary phenomena.

Hunt's acknowledgment of the limitless possibilities of poststructural theory in the Young Adult literature classroom coincides with an awareness on the part of many secondary pre-service teachers that poststructuralism offers high school teachers methods to help students access literature in ways that traditional New Critical readings might not. Poststructuralism's allowance of reader-centered readings, contextualized readings, deconstructive readings, and (re)visionary readings offers much hope for high school English teachers who are tired of discussing the whiteness of the whale in *Moby-Dick*. Some gifted teachers can use canonical readings of canonical texts to generate excitement among students, who are usually themselves also gifted. But I would not want to have to try it myself — so I offer now some theoretical perspectives on teaching YA literature in the hopes of contributing to the discussion about the place of poststructural theory in the English education classroom already begun by people like Bruce Pirie and Ray Linn.[1]

## Reader-Centered Readings

If there is one thing poststructuralism has offered critics that most liberates the adolescent reader, it is the concept of exactly that: the adolescent reader. Before critics like Wolfgang Iser and Stanley Fish started talking about the possibilities of multiple readings and implied readers, high school students were told too often that only one literary interpretation was "correct." As Patrocinio Schweickart observes, everyone was taught to read like a white male (adult). But articles like Anna Lawrence-Pietroni's analysis of Margaret Mahy's novels show how some authors allow for the possibility of a fluid reader, one who, in fact, might even be adolescent. Anita Tarr's phenomenological reading of Scott O'Dell's *Island of the Blue Dolphins* (1960) offers another perspective on the adolescent reader, one that employs strategies similar to

Schweickart's in teaching students how to refuse the position imposed on them by patriarchal texts like *Island of the Blue Dolphins*. Tarr uses Iser's concept of the "gap" to demonstrate how O'Dell relies on stereotypes to create a number of both racist and sexist lacunae for the reader to fill in. The significant thing in Tarr's work is how she provides students an alternative to the mind control that they experience when a text creates an implied reader who is sexist or racist.

Tarr's technique can be applied to Bruce Brooks's *The Moves Make the Man* (1984). With that novel, Bruce Brooks makes the same mistake that Scott O'Dell has in *Island of the Blue Dolphins*. The narrator of *The Moves Make the Man*, Jerome Foxworthy, is a black teenager. He feels compelled to explain black mores to his reader, most notably in an opening description where he explains black attitudes toward Little League. If Jerome's commentary were made specific to the culture of the town in which he lived, such explication would be less problematic. But as it is, he acts as if the reader has no knowledge of black culture. If the implied reader were black, such explanations would be unnecessary, so my students eventually arrive at the conclusion that *The Moves Make the Man* defines the reader as white, even though the narrator is black. Discussing a novel like this — especially in the context of Tarr's accessible descriptions of phenomenology and reader response theory — helps my students get past their reductive logic that "if the narrator is a white girl, the implied reader is a white girl; if the narrator is a black boy, the implied reader is a black boy." As they learn to identify and negotiate the textual gaps YA novels create, they learn to interrogate their own position as readers, and they become both more active readers and more socially aware.

Critics like Tarr who focus on the transaction between the text and the reader are so common in children's literature that I have adopted a mental label for them: I call theorists such as Peter Hollindale, Peter Hunt, Jill May, Rod McGillis, Maria Nikolajeva, Perry Nodelman, Lissa Paul, and John Stephens Transactional Critics. These critics have been leaders in asking readers of children's literature to be aware of how texts interact with their readers in a transaction that is both aesthetic and cultural. They are all influenced by poststructural criticism, and they all recognize the primacy of understanding the relationship between the adolescent reader and the text. Jill May formulates an underlying principle that motivates these critics: adolescents can only become active readers if they have been taught the skills required for active reading by professionals who understand the nuances of how texts operate (17).

## Contextualized Readings

Part of creating more culturally aware readers is creating more historically aware readers. Readers who understand themselves as contextually bound and who understand the historical context of what they read have a different understanding of a text than those who are isolated from such information. People who do not understand the Holocaust cannot possibly understand Anne Frank's *Diary*, so I give history lessons when I teach it. Even explaining the Great Depression helps students have (slightly) more tolerance for *Seventeenth Summer*. But such poststructural critics as Mitzi Myers and Lynne Vallone provide readers with even more intricate ways of understanding historical contextuality. Myers's "Impeccable Governesses, Rational Dames, and Moral Mothers," for example, gives an intellectual history of one of the first novels actually written for Young Adults, Mary Wollstonecraft's *Original Stories from Real Life* (1788). Lynne Vallone's *Disciplines of Virtue* helps readers understand how adolescent girls became the object of cultural ideological wars. Angela Estes and Kathleen Lant show how such ideological tensions lead that prototypical adolescent novel, *Little Women*, to deconstruct itself as Jo March diverts her anger at her culture's efforts to repress her into self-immolating anger at herself. Shirley Foster and Judy Simons also deconstruct *Little Women* within its historical context: they see the novel as representative of the "complexities that underlie essentialist concepts of definitive gendered identity" (104). And their argument — like Vallone's, like Myers's, like Estes and Lant's — is accessible to students seeking to understand the tensions between textuality and contextuality.

## Deconstructive Readings

It is no accident that much of the historical work done on adolescent literature is performed by revisionist feminists who rely on deconstructive methodology. Feminists understand that history has constructed adolescent gender politics in contradictory ways. Moreover, poststructural poetics allow for informed close readings that foreground such contradictions. And what could be more appropriate to a body of literature about inherently contradictory people (teenagers) than a literary strategy that surfaces contradictions? As a result, YA literary theorists have also discovered the relevance of Bakhtinian theory in deconstructing adolescent literature. As I indicated in Chapter 2, two of Bakhtin's concepts have almost perfect applicability in adolescent literature because of the very nature of the field. Maria Nikolajeva (99–102) and Michael Cadden ("Speaking" 516–519) discuss Bakhtin's concept of dialogic voices, competing narrative voices sometimes referred to as "heteroglossia" or "polyphony." Len Hatfield, too, has noted the complexity of shifting authority at work in such novels as *Tehanu* (52). Much of that novel is defined by competing concepts of who Tehanu is, as Cadden points out. Tehanu is at once child and not-child, dragon and not-dragon; she is wizard and not-wizard, and Cadden demonstrates how her amorphousness affects Tenar as the novel's focalizer ("Dialogues" 88–108).[2] One of the most fun exercises I have yet devised for helping students access dialogic voices is a role-playing exercise: one group can argue Tehanu's position, another Tenar's, another Ged's as I pose varied questions to them. When they have to answer as Ged or as Tehanu, they discover that each of these characters has more than one perspective, more than one voice. It is an easy way to define the difference between the "monologic" and "polyphony."

Michelle Martin shows polyphony at work in the competing voices that struggle to control most texts of menstrual education. She also discusses the second Bakhtinian concept I find useful in the YA classroom: his idea of the "carnivalesque," as John Stephens applies it to children's literature:

> Carnival laughter is the laughter of all the people. Second, it is universal in scope; it is directed at all and everyone, including

the carnival's participants. The entire world is seen in its droll aspect, in its gay relativity. Third, this laughter is ambivalent: it is gay, triumphant, and at the same time, mocking, deriding. It asserts and denies, it buries and revives. ("Rabelais and His World" 200; quoted in Martin, "Periods," Ph.D. diss. 6)

Martin acknowledges that the Bakhtinian concept of the medieval grotesque — a dark focus on the corporeal — combines easily with the carnivalesque in adolescent literature because of adolescents' extreme anxieties about their physical bodies ("Periods" 21). Martin's extended reading of the dialogics created by the carnivalesque grotesque in such novels as Mollie Hunter's *A Sound of Chariots* leaves open myriad possibilities for secondary teachers. What are the novels that celebrate — and protest — the human body? What novels both laugh and cry about the vicissitudes of adolescence? Novelists often dismissed by critics trying to legitimize the field are ripe for such Bakhtinian readings: Judy Blume, M. E. Kerr, Hadley Irwin, and Richard Peck could all be read as jesters parodying the adolescent body. Christian Peter Knoeller, in *Voicing Ourselves*, advocates such readings and demonstrates how effectively they can be implemented in high school classrooms.

Francesca Lia Block's novels intentionally capture competing dialogues that celebrate and mourn the human body. In *Weetzie Bat*, the gay character Duck fears AIDS but finds solace in making love with his boyfriend, Dirk; Weetzie wants to get pregnant but cannot without Max's support — until she finds another way to celebrate her fertility and sleeps with both Dirk and Duck. The moral dilemma Weetzie's actions create invokes a heteroglossia found in the culture at large: When Weetzie becomes pregnant, Max is angry; Dirk and Duck are delighted; and Weetzie herself is first full of anticipation, "like an Easter basket of pastel chocolate malt eggs and solid-milk-chocolate bunnies, and yellow daffodils and doll-house-sized jelly-bean eggs" (48). Later, however, she is just plain tired as she carries the "baby she felt rippling inside of her like a mermaid" (50). The text allows her both joy and fatigue, both pleasure and pain.

If in the process of reading *Weetzie Bat* students discover that its ideology is contradictory, then they have discovered both another level of the text's dialogics and another way to read literature. Linda Benson draws from John Stephens's modification of Genette's concept of the narrative focalizer when she analyzes the ideology of the literacy narrative at work in Katherine Paterson's *Lyddie*. Informed by Peter Hollindale, who is in turn informed by an Althusserian Marxism, Benson demonstrates how much students in the adolescent literature classroom have to gain when they can distinguish explicit ideologies from implicit ideologies. Less vulnerable to textual manipulation, more self-aware, and more aware of their students' ideologies, ideologically trained readers can deconstruct for themselves the competing ideologies in *Weetzie Bat*. Explicitly, the text exhorts societal acceptance of all love relationships, that we all "plug into the love current instead" (88). But implicitly, the text affirms the status quo, for Block does not rest easy until everyone in her novels is paired off, two by two, even if gender and orientation are irrelevant to her dyads. Students trained to read for competing dialogues intuit that in Block's novels, ultimately, nothing all that radical really happens.

## *(Re)visionary Readings*

Caroline Hunt notes that one of the most critical foci of the study of adolescent literature has been our involvement in responding to notions of canonicity. Anyone in the field necessarily deals with these issues: YA novels are, by definition, outside the traditional white male canon. Poststructuralism has given us many arguments for expanding the canon, and as a result, we have studies like Nancy Tolson's "Regional Outreach and an Evolving Black Aesthetic" that introduced me to Angela Johnson's *Toning the Sweep* in 1994. I have used the novel numerous times since then to teach two things: historical contextualization (which students gain as we talk about the Civil Rights movement when one character is lynched by a racist mob) and feminism (which we talk about in terms of the female community created by the narrator, her mother, and her grandmother as they grieve communally the elder woman's dying). Several of the strategies I have already discussed work beautifully as we discuss multicultural narratives such as those by Virginia Hamilton, Laurence Yep, Walter Dean Myers, Minfong Ho, or Gary Soto. We can talk about competing voices — intraracially or interracially. We can talk about competing ideologies — explicit ones or implicit ones. We can talk about discourses of power, historical contextualization, how various multicultural novels create implied readers, aporias and how they are overcome, or even how the aesthetics in novels by authors of color are different from and similar to aesthetics by Euro-American authors.

We also talk about the conjunction between race and gender as a function of how empowerment is tied to discourse. I encourage my students to look at all the factors of positive feminism at work in a novel like *Toning the Sweep*: not just the female community, but the narrator's sense of agency her voice, and her choices (Trites, *Waking Sleeping Beauty* 37–39). In more metafictional novels like *Tehanu* and *Weetzie Bat*, we can talk about the self-conscious narrative strategies the author employs to engage the reader in understanding her female characters' power. Lissa Paul's *Reading Otherways* is a text designed to engage undergraduates in thinking about feminist theory. I have also found Virginia Schaefer Carroll's rubric for analyzing feminist fiction particularly effective in the adolescent literature classroom: she investigates how Maureen Daly's *Seventeenth Summer* is about female education, female identify formation, female voice, and female choice (13). After we talk about how Carol Gilligan's concept of female identity formation occurs within a complicated network of interrelationships, we can analyze these four factors in novels as diverse as Sylvia Engdahl's *Enchantress from the Stars* and Sparks's *It Happened to Nancy*. Carroll's article provides my students with a key to unlocking the complex spectrum that ranges from sexism to feminism — and in the process of the discussions, many of my students, both male and female, discover to their amusement and sometimes horror that they are themselves feminists.

Karen Coats's "Lacan for Runt Pigs" and Roderick McGillis's "Another Kick at La/can" are comprehensible guides to Lacanian psychoanalytic theory useful to theorists of the YA novel. Furthermore, Coats's readings of *The Chocolate War* and L'Engle's *A Wrinkle in Time* (1962) particularize YA novels as a genre informed by the adolescent's phallic crisis ("Performing the Subject" 142–176). Kenneth Kidd's introduction to the fall 1998 *Children's Literature Association Quarterly* has a superb introduction to queer discourse in adolescent literature, and Vanessa Wayne Lee's "'Unshelter Me'" in the same issue provides an introduction to lesbian theory and adolescent narratives (152–159). Peter Hollindale's *Signs of Childness in Children's Books* is excellent for — among other things — its chapter that contains an interesting reading of adolescent literature. Like many of the Transactional Critics, Hollindale believes that helping adolescents access literature can change the world for the better.

The important thing to me in the revolution that has occurred in the last twenty years of the study of YA literature is the degree of dialogue that informs the field. Our students have benefited from this dialogue, and so will their students in turn. I am not afraid of anyone getting theoretical in the high school classroom. I am far more afraid of monologic teacher education than I am of polyphonic teacher education. Our ability to teach theoretically is revitalizing a once moribund field. Nothing has greater potential for disturbing the universe of literary criticism for the good of ourselves, our students, and their students — the adolescent readers who, when all is said and done, are the ones who matter most in this dialogue.

# Notes

1. This despite Aidan Chambers' observation that the identity crisis is a phenomenon of middle age, not adolescence, for adolescents still do not have a full sense of their own identity (Chambers, "All of a Tremble" 198).

2. Several critics deal with the issue of home in children's literature. See, for example, Michael J. Cadden's "Home is a Matter of Blood, Time, and Genre"; Christopher Clausen's "Home and Away in Children's Fiction"; Perry Nodelman's *The Pleasures of Children's Literature*; Jon Stott and Christine Doyle Francis's "'Home' and 'Not Home' in Children's Stories: Getting There—and Being Worth It"; and Lucy Waddey's "Homes in Children's Fiction: Three Patterns." The third chapter of Cadden's dissertation, "Dialogues with Authority: Children's Literature, Dialogics, and the Texts of Ursula K. Le Guin," provides a summative analysis of these descriptions of the use of home in children's literature in terms of ideology and narrative structure. See also his "Speaking Across the Spaces Between Us."

3. Foucault defines all power as a social imperative that invariably produces something: "By power, I do not mean 'Power' as a group of institutions and mechanisms that ensure the subservience of the citizens of a given state. By power, I do not mean, either, a mode of subjugation which, in contrast to violence, has the form of the rule. Finally, I do not have in mind a general system of domination exerted by one group over another, a system whose effects, through successive derivations, pervade the entire social body. . . . It seems to me that power must be understood in the first instance as the multiplicity of force relations immanent in the sphere in which they operate and which constitute their own organization; as the process which, through ceaseless struggles and confrontations, transforms, strengthens or reverses them; as the support which these force relations find in one another . . . and lastly, as the strategies in which they take effect, whose general design or institutional crystallization is embodied in the state apparatus, in the formulation of the law, in the various social hegemonies" (*History* 92–93).

4. Australian sociologist R. W. Connell notes that "power may be a balance of advantage or an inequality of resources in a workplace, a household, or a larger institution" (107).

5. The concept of subjectivity assumes that every individual is multiply constructed by a variety of sociolinguistic forces that act on her or him. Assuming a subject position (as opposed to an object position) is a matter of engaging one's agency. (For an assessment of this process that is specific to children's and adolescent literature, see Trites, *Waking Sleeping Beauty* 26–29.)

6. Coats defines *"assomption"* relying on Lacan's use of the term as: "the taking on oneself the position heretofore merely ascribed to her by the Other" ("Performing the Subject" 41). For her extended analysis of *The Chocolate War*, see "Performing the Subject" 169–174.

7. Kenneth Donelson and Alleen Pace Nilsen somewhat inconsistently define YA literature in terms of what people between the "ages of 12 and 20 choose to read (as opposed to what they may be coerced to read for class assignments)," but employ market-driven publishers' lists to define children's literature: "When we talk about *children's literature*, we refer to books released by the juvenile or junior divisions of a publisher and intended for children from prekindergarten to about sixth grade" (6).

8. Caroline Hunt (5) and Ben F. Nelms (9) cite 1942 and 1967. Richard Peck (19–20) and Michael Cart (156) cite 1967. Poe, Samuels, and Carter name 1968, which they accurately cite as the publication date of *The Pigman* and which they inaccurately cite as the publication date of *The Outsiders* (65). Geraldine DeLuca defines *The Catcher in the Rye* as "the one book that the adolescent novel comes from" ("Unself-Conscious Voices" 89). Maria Nikolajeva also considers it a ground-breaking novel (66), and Lukens and Cline describe it as the novel that most completely addresses the issues of adolescent literature (171).

9. Dagmar Grenz provides a perspective on the German adolescent novel as a genre in which the "young hero . . . is in the midst of an existential crisis" (173).

10. For a thorough overview of the history of youth literature, see Donelson and Nilsen (413–440).

11. See, for example, Brown and Stephens (18).

12. Tennyson consciously collapses the categories of *Bildungsroman* and *Entwicklungsroman* into one category because he perceives the spiritual element that the Victorians added to the British *Bildungsroman* when Romantic optimism began to dissipate as *the* crucial element of the Victorian *Bildungsroman* (144). In the final sentence of a paper he gave in 1968 that fixed the Anglo-American definition of the novel of development, Tennyson elides the term *Entwicklungsroman* with the term *Bildungsroman*, saying: "If such a conception [of uniform spiritual *Bildung* in the Victorian novel] can be affirmed as the true common ground of Victorian novels of development, then we have returned to something close to Dilthey's concept [of the goal of the *Bildungsroman* being a blend of learning to balance the material and the spiritual worlds], and have found that the English *Entwicklungsroman* is also the English *Bildungsroman*" (145). The two terms have been used as one more often than not for the thirty years that followed Tennyson's presentation.

13. G. B. Tennyson considers the English *Bildungsroman* "Victorian rather than Romantic because it takes its rise from the work in the eighteen-twenties of that later-to-be eminent Victorian Thomas Carlyle," who translated *Wilhelm Meister* into English (139). I am less convinced than Tennyson that Victorianism is a literary phase distinct from Romanticism.

14. See chapter 5 of Linda Benson's dissertation, "The Constructed Child," for more on literacy narratives in adolescent literature.

15. The message, a lovely one for modern readers, is perhaps not the most accurate representation of what a nineteenth-century young woman's emotional life might have been like.

16. According to Foucault, "discourse" is a concept inseparable from "language" as a concept. If language is "the concrete link between representation and reflection," then discourse is the "sequence of verbal signs," the movement between linguistic signs that makes meaning possible (Foucault, *Order* 83). Thus, "discourse" is the interaction of language systems by means of which communication occurs.

17. I generally use "postmodernism" to refer to the era and its artistic products and "poststructuralism" to refer to literary theories that follow structuralism.

CHAPTER 2

1. Fredric Jameson traces the connection between ideology and Lacan's concept of the Symbolic; ideology is inescapable because of our complete immersion in the Symbolic Order (*Postmodernism* 53–54).

2. According to Henry Littlefield, Baum was a populist who wrote *The Wonderful Wizard of Oz* to reflect his political agendas, such as including silver along with gold in the monetary base and advocating for workers' and farmers' rights. Thus, Littlefield interprets the yellow brick road as bricks of gold; silver shoes walk on them to lead the way to the Emerald City, the green city of money, Washington, D.C. (53). In this taxonomy, the Munchkins are little and blue because they represent the repressed blue-collar workers of the East, and the Native Americans have been imprisoned as the Winged Monkeys in the West — whose ills can only be cured by killing the Wicked Witch of the West with water: irrigation. The scarecrow is the farmer who thinks he does not have a brain but does; the Tin Woods-man is industry that has eventually become so mechanized that it is heartless; the Cowardly Lion is William Jennings Bryant, the Populists' favorite candidate; and the Wizard is the humbug president of the United States, William McKinley.

3. Isabel Quigly identifies several factors that led to girls' school stories being a later literary phenomenon than boys' school stories, including the fact that girls' boarding schools were established in England as a cultural institution later than boys' boarding schools and the fact that upper-class girls were more likely to be educated at home by governesses than were their male coun-

terparts (213). Mitzi Myers's "Reading Children and Homeopathic Romanticism" (55–56) and Cadogan and Craig's *You're A Brick, Angela!* (111–124) also add to the discussion of gender in school stories. See also R. Moore (378–379) and Richards (2).

4. In "The Grotesque and the Taboo in Roald Dahl's Humorous Writings for Children," Mark West provides a synthesis of Freud's theory of humor as it influences several theoreticians exploring humor. See also David Monro's *Argument of Laughter.*

5. Similarly, Nikolajeva perceives children's literature as a more polyphonic literature since the 1960s because of an increased cultural awareness of children's subjectivity (99–102).

6. See also Elizabeth Janeway's *Man's World, Woman's Place* (8–10); Hélène Cixous's "The Laugh of the Medusa"; Mary Daly's *Gyn/Ecology* (1–22); and the first chapter of Judith Butler's *Gender Trouble.*

7. For a standard definition of essentialism see Irena R. Makaryk's definition in the *Encyclopedia of Contemporary Literary Theory*: "the valorization of 'woman's' biological or cultural essence" (545).

8. For more on silencing in the Logan family books, see Trites, *Waking Sleeping Beauty* 49–51.

CHAPTER 3

1. Karen Coats provides a Lacanian explanation for this process in "Lacan with Runt Pigs."

2. Marilyn Frye describes how Lacan's theory is dependent upon Saussurean concepts of linguistics: "the elements [of language] are constituted by what they are not. Or, even more paradoxically: an element is constituted by the-absence-of-it. . . . In this world, to be is to be a signifier, and a signifier is construed as 'that which is constituted by the-absence-of-it.' And now, all one has to do is acknowledge the 'obvious,' that the phallus is also 'that which is constituted by the contrast with the-absence-of-it,' and one can see that the signifier is the phallus and the phallus is the signifier. The subject is a signifier, so it follows that the subject must be the phallus" (994).

3. Marilyn Frye provides an eloquent gender-based critique of Lacan in "The Necessity of Differences."

4. Ann B. Murphy, for example, notes that "much of *Little Women*'s power derives from its exploration of the previously repressed, complex mother-daughter relationship, without portraying that bond as either idealized perfection or pernicious destruction" (575).

5. For a clear delineation of Jo's self-evisceration, see Estes and Lant's "Dismembering the Text: The Horror of Louisa May Alcott's *Little Women*." Foster and Simon interpret the infamous hair-cutting scene "in Freudian terms as a re-enactment of the experience of female castration. Jo's recogni-

tion of lack is commensurate with her loss of innocence and exposes her fear of initiation into adult sexuality" (96).

6. *Seventeenth Summer* has been called the first young adult novel and has been held responsible for stimulating the publishing industry's attention to the genre: "the adolescent novel as we know it may be said to have sprung from the popularity and seriousness of Maureen Daly's *Seventeenth Summer*" (Nelms 9). See the 1992 issue of *English Journal* (vol. 81, no. 4), which is dedicated to adolescent literature.

7. In fact, as Karen Coats once commented to me, the Demeter-Persephone myth may be a more appropriate interpretation of both these novels: Jo views John Brooke as the Hades who has stolen Persephone from her, and in *Seventeenth Summer*, Jack serves as the Hades who steals the Persephone-like Angie for one sensual summer.

8. One of the most positive effects of feminism on adolescent literature is that female rebellion against present parents has been taken more seriously in books published since the mid-1980s: Crescent Dragonwagon's *The Year It Rained* and Barbara Wersba's *Love Is the Crooked Thing* (1987) demonstrate girls who rebel against their parents eventually gaining autonomy without denying their mothers. See Trites, *Waking Sleeping Beauty*, 89–91, 104–106.

9. The gender of the parent is not strictly defined; mothers can serve as symbolic fathers. Melanin Sun's mother provides one such example.

10. Lacan, of course, would argue that the actual is entirely determined by the Symbolic Order. As Lacan's translator Alan Sheridan notes, "The symbolic . . . is . . . the determining order of the subject" (*Écrits* ix).

11. The pre-Oedipal stage is the stage when the infant believes itself still to be in Imaginary oneness with its mother (Lacan, *Écrits* 1–7, 197–199). For a concise explanation and an elegant application to another adolescent text, see Roni Natov's essay on *Annie John*.

12. Bob Dixon first asked scholars of children's and adolescent literature to investigate textual ideologies in his two-volume work *Catching Them Young*. Bob Sutherland also classifies explicit ideology in children's literature as "the politics of advocacy [and] the politics of attack" and implicit ideological assumptions as "the politics of assent" (145), but neither Dixon nor Sutherland complicates the issues of ideology as much as Hollindale does.

13. The text is quite explicit that in groups, teenagers have power that is both constructive and destructive. Grace needs another teenager to help her heal because she has been sexually assaulted by a group of her peers.

14. For an assessment of the irony inherent in the use of the first-person narrator in books written for adolescents, see Michael J. Cadden's "Ironic Tension in the Young Adult Novel."

15. See also Susan S. Lanser, "Toward a Feminist Narratology," and Trites, "'I double'" (148–149).

16. Patrocinio Schweickart demonstrates how patriarchal constructs seduce the reading subject into an identity as white, male (and adult) and ad-

vocates feminist counterreadings that do not require the reader to efface herself (31–62).

17. Judith Fetterley advocates that women read as "resisting" readers who refuse to participate in the totalizing discourse of patriarchal literature (xxii); black readers who refuse to adopt white subject positions are also resisting readers.

18. Adolescent novels share with picture books and children's novels a history grounded in educating children, so the didactic impulse in many of the books in these genres is not surprising.

### CHAPTER 4

1. As Kate Soper notes: "It is one thing to argue that we do not have experience of the body other than as symbolically and culturally mediated; it is quite another to suggest that bodies are 'constructed' out of cultural forces in the same manner that, say, telephones are put together" (32). She points out two important differences: bodies exist physically before any cultural act has shaped them, and unlike telephones, bodies are never completely constructed. They continue to change and grow throughout time, which is where Foucault's point about cultural influences becomes, of course, most important (32).

See also Bailey 116; Bartky 64; Ramazanoglu 4–8; McNay 3, 11–47; Weeks 223.

2. Judy Blume's *Deenie* (1973) includes a validation of masturbation; her *Then Again, Maybe I Won't* (1971) includes a validation of nocturnal emissions; her *Forever* validates teenagers' desire to have intercourse.

3. Characters in *Edith Jackson* and *My Darling, My Hamburger* both undergo abortions without the support of their male partners.

4. "*Jouissance*" can be defined as sexual rapture, as an orgasmic experience that is beyond language.

5. There is a certain irony in my describing L'Engle's writing in poststructural terms: L'Engle asserts in *A House Like a Lotus* that people have a unique and inherent inner quality that poststructuralism's insistence on the primacy of language in determining subjectivity precludes. When Polly's friend Max asks her, "So, what is it, this thing called soul?" Polly answers, "It's — it's your *you* and my *me*. . . . It's what makes us *us*, different from anybody else in the world. . . . The soul isn't — ephemeral" (181–182, emphasis in the original). Max replies, "So it's us, at our highest and least self-conscious" (182). Their conversation demonstrates the humanist belief in the inviolability of the human soul — a concept largely antithetical to poststructuralist theories.

6. Following the impulse of Queer Theory to claim for itself a pejorative term and transform it into something positive, I refer to YA novels about characters whose sexual orientation involves same-sex partners as "queer YA novels."

CHAPTER 5

1. For Heidegger, "Being-towards-death" represents the moment of maturation in which the subject defines himself in terms of his own death, in terms of his own not being (304–307). See also Coats, "Lacan" 106.

2. Margaret Atwood's *Bodily Harm* (1981), Marilyn French's *Her Mother's Daughter* (1987), Ann Beattie's *Picturing Will* (1989), Jamaica Kincaid's *Lucy* (1990), and Amy Tan's *The Hundred Secret Senses* (1995), for example, are novels that depict women developing their own sense of personal power through photography. Since women's literature shares with adolescent literature a concern for people who initially feel disempowered but grow into an increased awareness of what exactly agency entails, it seems natural that the metaphor of the camera recurs as often in adolescent literature as it does in women's literature.

3. In the process of aiding protagonists to explore their agency and achieve resolution, cameras and photographs provide literary characters with a number of emotional experiences. Sharon R. Wilson notes that Margaret Atwood uses photography for four purposes: to give characters "'neutral' recorders of experience"; to demonstrate "a character's sense of fragmentation"; to provide that character with "proof" of her own existence; and to provide "lenses which distill and focus experience, facilitating a self-discovery which transcends mere 'self-surveillance'" (31–32). The three novels I discuss herein employ these four patterns to varying degrees, but the pattern of photography as a catalyst for transcendence is the most noteworthy.

4. I share an interest with Barthes and Hirsch in photographs of people rather than of landscapes or inanimate objects.

5. Barthes writes, "A specific photograph, in effect, is never distinguished from its referent (from what it represents), or at least it is not *immediately* or *generally* distinguished from its referent (as is the case for every other image, encumbered — from the start, and because of its status — by the way in which the object is simulated): it is not impossible to perceive the photographic signifier . . . but it requires a secondary action of knowledge or of reflection" (5, emphasis in the original).

6. Hirsch defines it this way: "The referent is both present (implied in the photograph) and absent (it has been there but is not here now)" (5). Hirsch even uses photography as the metaphor whereby she explains signification in language, connecting the process to the fluidity of social power: "The triangular field in which signifier, signified, and interpreting subject interact in the process of symbolization is much like the triangular field of the photograph, in which the photographer, the object, and the viewer interrelate through imaginary projections they more or less share. Power, in this structure of play, is not unidimensional or unidirectional: it circulates in multiple ways within the process of taking, developing, assembling, and reading pictures and within the social space and the historical moment in which photography operates"

(176). Barthes's description of the photograph synthesizes the dichotomy between signifier and signified that Hirsch is describing: the photograph is for the viewer, at least initially, signifier and signified, just as it can contain the paradoxical image of a communicating subject that has become an object (5).

7. Deborah Bowen identifies Sontag's definition of photography as differing epistemologically from Barthes's approach to photography: Sontag views pictures as a means to an end, as a way of coming to some sort of understanding; Barthes celebrates photos as an end in themselves; he values what the photograph reveals far more than he values what the photographer or viewer has learned in the process of taking or observing the picture. As Bowen puts it, Sontag privileges "function" and Barthes "form" (21).

8. Or, in other terms, her camera is *langue*, her pictures *parole*.

9. For a lucid explanation of Lacanian theory as it applies to photography, see Hirsch (101–103).

10. Photography as elegy is a leitmotif in Hirsch's *Family Frames*. Not only does Hirsch cite this quotation from Barthes (quoted in Hirsch 175), but she also quotes Marguerite Duras's statement, "The fixed, flat, easily available countenance of a dead person or an infant in a photograph is only one image as against the million images that exist in the mind. And the sequence made up by the million images will never alter. It's a confirmation of death" (quoted in Hirsch 200) and Susan Sontag's statements: "All photographs are *memento mori*" (quoted in Hirsch 17) and "this link between photography and death haunts all photos of people" (quoted in Hirsch 19). According to Hirsch, "The referent [of a photograph] haunts the picture like a ghost: it is a revenant, a return of the lost and dead other" (5) and the photographic still is a "deathlike fixing of one moment in time" (24).

11. Julia Kristeva, in fact, links all linguistic constructions, linear as they are, with death: "It might also be added that this linear time is that of language considered as the enunciation of sentences (noun + verb; topic-comment; beginning-ending), and that this time rests on its own stumbling block, which is also the stumbling block of that enunciation — death" (17).

12. Brooks bases his theory on Freud's essay "Beyond the Pleasure Principle," demonstrating how, "If beginning is desire, and is ultimately desire for the end, between lies a process" that Brooks links to plot production ("Freud's Masterplot" 284). He maintains that "the sense of the beginning, then, is determined by the sense of an ending" ("Freud's Masterplot" 283), for "all narration is obituary in that life acquires definable meaning only at, and through, death" ("Freud's Masterplot" 284). In the revised version of this essay that appears as a chapter in *Reading for the Plot*, Brooks embellishes this statement: "All narrative may be in essence obituary in that . . . the retrospective knowledge that it seeks, the knowledge that comes after, stands on the far side of the end, in human terms on the far side of death" (95). For a trenchant critique of what is masculinist in Brooks's argument, see Susan Winnett's article, "Coming Unstrung."

13. As Peter Brooks says of similar narrative repetitions in *Great Expecta-*

*tions,* "repetition and return have spoken of the death instinct, the drive to return to the quiescence of the inorganic, of the nontextual. Yet the repetitions . . . both prolonging the detour and more effectively preparing the final discharge, have created that delay necessary to incorporate the past within the present and to let us understand end in relation to beginning" (*Reading for the Plot* 139).

CHAPTER 6

1. Henry Giroux and Steven R. Chisnell have also contributed to this dialogue.

2. John Stephens employs the term "focalizer" to indicate a narrative persona whose perspective focuses the reader's attention (27).

# Bibliography

LITERARY WORKS

Alcott, Louisa May. *Little Women*. 1868, 1869. Boston: Little, Brown, 1968.
Atwood, Margaret. *Bodily Harm*. New York: Toronto: McClelland and Stewart, 1981.
Avi. *Nothing but the Truth: A Documentary Novel*. New York: Orchard, 1991.
Baum, L. Frank. *The Wonderful Wizard of Oz*. 1900. New York: Dover, 1960.
Beattie, Ann. *Picturing Will*. New York: Random House, 1989.
Bennett, James. *I Can Hear the Mourning Dove*. Boston: Houghton-Mifflin, 1990.
Block, Francesca Lia. *Baby Be-Bop*. New York: HarperCollins, 1995.
———. *The Hanged Man*. New York: HarperCollins, 1994.
———. *Weetzie Bat*. New York: HarperCollins, 1989.
———. *Witch Baby*. New York: HarperCollins, 1991.
Blume, Judy. *Deenie*. Scarsdale, N.Y.: Bradbury, 1973.
———. *Forever*. New York: Simon and Schuster, 1975.
———. *Then Again, Maybe I Won't*. Scarsdale, N.Y.: Bradbury, 1971.
Brooks, Bruce. *The Moves Make the Man*. New York: Harper and Row, 1984.
Chambers, Aidan. *Breaktime*. New York: Harper and Row, 1978.
———. *Dance on My Grave*. New York: Harper and Row, 1982.
Chbosky, Stephen. *The Perks of Being a Wallflower*. New York: Simon and Schuster, 1999.
Clemens, Samuel. *Adventures of Huckleberry Finn*. 1885. New York: Signet, 1959.
Collier, James Lincoln, and Christopher Collier. *My Brother Sam Is Dead*. New York: Scholastic, 1974.
Conford, Ellen. *To All My Fans, with Love, from Sylvie*. Boston: Little, Brown, 1982.
Cormier, Robert. *The Chocolate War*. New York: Dell, 1974.
———. *I Am the Cheese*. New York: Dell, 1977.
Cross, Gillian. *Pictures in the Dark*. New York: Holiday House, 1996.
Crutcher, Chris. *Ironman*. New York: Greenwillow, 1995.
———. *Running Loose*. New York: Greenwillow, 1983.

———. *Staying Fat for Sarah Byrnes.* 1993. New York: Dell, 1995.

Daly, Maureen. *Seventeenth Summer.* New York: Dodd, 1942.

Donovan, John. *I'll Get There. It Better Be Worth the Trip.* New York: Harper and Row, 1969.

Dragonwagon, Crescent. *The Year It Rained.* New York: Macmillan, 1985.

Eliot, T. S. "The Love Song of J. Alfred Prufrock." *The Complete Poems and Plays, 1909–1950.* New York: Harcourt, Brace and World, 1952.

Engdahl, Sylvia. *Enchantress from the Stars.* New York: Atheneum, 1970.

Forbes, Esther. *Johnny Tremain.* Boston: Houghton-Mifflin, 1943.

Frank, Anne. *Anne Frank: The Diary of a Young Girl.* Garden City, N.Y.: Doubleday, 1952.

French, Marilyn. *Her Mother's Daughter.* New York: Summit, 1987.

Garden, Nancy. *Good Moon Rising.* New York: Farrar, Straus, Giroux, 1996.

Grimsley, Jim. *Dream Boy.* Chapel Hill: Algonquin, 1995.

Guy, Rosa. *Edith Jackson.* New York: Viking, 1978.

Hamilton, Virginia. *Arilla Sun Down.* New York: Greenwillow, 1976.

———. *The Gathering.* New York: Greenwillow, 1981.

———. *M. C. Higgins, the Great.* New York: Macmillan, 1974.

———. *The Planet of Junior Brown.* New York: Macmillan, 1971.

———. *A White Romance.* New York: Philomel, 1987.

Hesse, Karen. *Out of the Dust.* New York: Scholastic, 1997.

Hinton, S. E. *The Outsiders.* New York: Dell, 1967.

———. *That Was Then, This Is Now.* New York: Dell, 1971.

Hunter, Mollie. *A Sound of Chariots.* New York: Harper and Row, 1972.

Irwin, Hadley. *Abby, My Love.* New York: Atheneum, 1985.

Johnson, Angela. *Toning the Sweep.* New York: Orchard, 1993.

Kerr, M. E. *Deliver Us from Evie.* New York: HarperCollins, 1994.

———. *Is That You, Miss Blue?* New York: Harper and Row, 1975.

———. *What I Really Think of You.* New York: Signet, 1982.

Kincaid, Jamaica. *Annie John.* New York: Farrar, Straus, Giroux, 1983.

———. *Lucy.* New York: Farrar, Straus, Giroux, 1990.

Klein, Norma. *It's OK if You Don't Love Me.* New York: Dial, 1977.

Knowles, John. *A Separate Peace.* New York: Macmillan, 1959.

Krisher, Trudy. *Spite Fences.* New York: Delacorte, 1994.

Larsen, Nella. *Passing.* New York: Knopf, 1929.

Lee, Harper. *To Kill a Mockingbird.* Philadelphia: Lippincott, 1960.

Le Guin, Ursula K. *The Beginning Place.* New York: Harper and Row, 1980.

———. *Tehanu.* New York: Macmillan, 1990.

———. *A Wizard of Earthsea.* 1968. New York: Bantam, 1975.

L'Engle, Madeleine. *A House Like a Lotus.* New York: Farrar, Straus, Giroux, 1984.

———. *A Swiftly Tilting Planet.* New York: Farrar, Straus, Giroux, 1978.

———. *A Wrinkle in Time.* New York: Farrar, Straus, Giroux, 1962.

Lowry, Lois. *The Giver.* Boston: Houghton-Mifflin, 1993.

———. *Number the Stars*. Boston: Houghton-Mifflin, 1989.

———. *A Summer to Die*. Boston: Houghton-Mifflin, 1977.

Mahy, Margaret. *The Changeover*. New York: Scholastic, 1984.

Marshall, Catherine. *Christy*. New York: McGraw-Hill, 1967.

Myers, Walter Dean. *Scorpions*. New York: Harper and Row, 1988.

O'Dell, Scott. *Island of the Blue Dolphins*. Boston: Houghton-Mifflin, 1960.

Paterson, Katherine. *Bridge to Terabithia*. New York: Harper and Row, 1977.

———. *The Great Gilly Hopkins*. New York: Crowell, 1978.

———. *Lyddie*. New York: Dutton, 1991.

Pinkwater, Daniel. *Alan Mendelsohn, the Boy from Mars*. New York: Dutton, 1979.

Pohl, Peter. *Johnny, My Friend*. 1985. Trans. Laurie Thompson. London: Turton and Chambers, 1991.

Potok, Chaim. *The Chosen*. New York: Simon and Schuster, 1967.

Rowling, J. K. *Harry Potter and the Chamber of Secrets*. New York: Scholastic, 1998.

———. *Harry Potter and the Prisoner of Azkaban*. New York: Scholastic, 1999.

———. *Harry Potter and the Sorcerer's Stone*. New York: Scholastic, 1997.

Salinger, J. D. *The Catcher in the Rye*. Boston: Little, Brown, 1951.

Sleator, William. *House of Stairs*. New York: Dutton, 1974.

Smith, Betty. *A Tree Grows in Brooklyn*. New York: Harper and Brothers, 1943.

Sparks, Beatrice. *Go Ask Alice*. Englewood Cliffs: Prentice-Hall, 1971.

———. *It Happened to Nancy*. New York: Avon, 1994.

Tan, Amy. *The Hundred Secret Senses*. New York: Putnam, 1995.

Taylor, Mildred. *The Road to Memphis*. New York: Dial, 1990.

Townsend, Sue. *The Secret Diary of Adrian Mole, Aged 13¾*. New York: Avon, 1982.

Voigt, Cynthia. *David and Jonathan*. New York: Scholastic, 1992.

———. *Dicey's Song*. New York: Atheneum, 1982.

———. *On Fortune's Wheel*. New York: Fawcett Juniper, 1990.

———. *The Homecoming*. New York: Atheneum, 1981.

———. *When She Hollers*. New York: Scholastic, 1994.

Webster, Jean. *Daddy-Long-Legs*. 1912. New York: Puffin, 1989.

Wersba, Barbara. *Love Is the Crooked Thing*. New York: Harper and Row, 1987.

Wilder, Laura Ingalls. *The Little Town on the Prairie*. Eau Claire, Wisc.: Hale, 1941.

———. *The Long Winter*. Eau Claire, Wisc.: Hale, 1940.

Wollstonecraft, Mary. *Original Stories from Real Life*. 1791. New York: Woodstock, 1990.

Woodson, Jacqueline. *From the Notebooks of Melanin Sun*. New York: Scholastic, 1995.

Yep, Laurence. *Dragonwings*. New York: Harper and Row, 1975.

Zindel, Paul. *David and Della*. New York: HarperCollins, 1993.

———. *My Darling, My Hamburger*. New York: Harper and Row, 1969.

———. *The Pigman*. New York: Bantam, 1968.

CRITICAL WORKS

Abel, Elizabeth, Marianne Hirsch, and Elizabeth Langland. *The Voyage In: Fictions of Female Development*. Hanover, N.H.: University Press of New England, 1983.

Althusser, Louis. "Ideology and Ideological State Apparatuses." In *Lenin and Philosophy and Other Essays*, translated by Ben Brewster, 127–186. New York: Monthly Review P, 1971.

Ammon, Richard. "Last Rites for the Young Adult Novel." *Journal of Children's Literature* 21.1 (1995): 61–62.

Angelotti, Michael. "Will There *Be* an Adolescent Literature in the 21st Century?" *ALAN Review* 7 (1979): 2.

Ariès, Philippe. *Western Attitudes to Death from the Middle Ages to the Present*. Baltimore: Johns Hopkins UP, 1974.

Aronson, Marc. "'The YA Novel is Dead' and Other Fairly Stupid Tales." *School Library Journal* (January 1995): 36–37.

Bailey, M. E. "Foucauldian Feminism: Contesting Bodies, Sexuality and Identity." In *Up Against Foucault: Explorations of Some Tensions between Foucault and Feminism*, edited by Caroline Ramazanoglu, 99–122. New York: Routledge, 1993.

Bakhtin, Mikhail. *The Dialogic Imagination: Four Essays by M. M. Bakhtin*. Edited by Michael Holquist and translated by Caryl Emerson and Michael Holquist. Austin: U of Texas P, 1981.

———. "Rabelais and His World." *The Bakhtin Reader*. Edited by Pam Morris, 195–206. New York: Routledge, 1994.

Banta, Martha. *Imaging American Women: Idea and Ideals in Cultural History*. New York: Columbia UP, 1987.

Barthes, Roland. *Camera Lucida: Reflections on Photography*. Translated by Richard Howard. New York: Hill and Wang, 1981.

Bartky, Sandra Lee. "Foucault, Femininity and the Modernisation of Patriarchal Power." In *Feminism and Foucault: Reflections on Resistance*, edited by Irene Diamond and Lee Quinby, 61–86. Boston: Northeastern UP, 1988.

Bedell, Madelon. *The Alcotts: Biography of a Family*. New York: Potter, 1980.

Belsey, Catharine. "Constructing the Subject: Deconstructing the Text." In *Feminist Criticism and Social Change*, edited by J. Newton and D. Rosenfelt, 45–64. London: Methuen, 1985.

Bennett, Tony. *Formalism and Marxism*. London: Methuen, 1979.

Benson, Linda. "The Constructed Child: Femininity in Beverly Cleary's Ramona Series." Ph.D. diss., Illinois State University, 1997.

Bergman, David. *Gaiety Transfigured: Gay Self-Representation in American Literature*. Madison: U of Wisconsin P, 1991.

Bishop, Rudine Sims. "Books from Parallel Cultures: Celebrating a Silver Anniversary." *Horn Book* (March-April 1993): 175–81.

Blume, Judy. *Letters to Judy: What Your Kids Wish They Could Tell You.* New York: Putnam, 1986.

Bowen, Deborah. "In Camera: The Developed Photographs of Margaret Laurence and Alice Munro." *Studies in Canadian Literature* 13 (1988): 20–33.

Brooks, Peter. "Freud's Masterplot." *Yale French Studies* 55/56 (1977): 280–300.

———. *Reading for the Plot: Design and Intention in Narrative.* New York: Knopf, 1984.

Brown, Jean E., and Elaine C. Stephens. *Teaching Young Adult Literature: Sharing the Connection.* Belmont: Wadsworth, 1995.

Buckley, Jerome. *Season of Youth: The Bildungsroman from Dickens to Golding.* Cambridge: Harvard UP, 1974.

Butler, Judith. *Gender Trouble: Feminism and the Subversion of Identity.* London: Routledge, 1990.

———. *The Psychic Life of Power.* Stanford: Stanford UP, 1997.

Cadden, Michael J. "Dialogues with Authority: Children's Literature, Dialogics, and the Texts of Ursula K. Le Guin." Ph.D. diss., Illinois State University, 1996.

———. "Home is a Matter of Blood, Time, and Genre: Essentialism in Burnett and McKinley." *ARIEL: A Review of International English Literature* 28.1 (January 1997): 53–67.

———. "Ironic Tension in the Young Adult Novel." Midwest Modern Language Association, St. Louis, November 5, 1998.

———. "Speaking Across the Spaces Between Us: Ursula Le Guin's Dialogic Use of Character in Children's and Adult Literature." *Paradoxa: Studies in World Literary Genres* 2 (1996): 516–530.

Cadogan, Mary, and Patricia Craig. *You're a Brick, Angela! A New Look at Girls' Fiction from 1839 to 1975.* London: Gollancz, 1976.

Campbell, Patricia J. *Presenting Robert Cormier.* Boston: Twayne, 1985.

Carroll, Virginia Schaefer. "Re-Reading the Romance of *Seventeenth Summer.*" *Children's Literature Association Quarterly* 21 (1996): 12–19.

Cart, Michael. "Of Risk and Revelation: The Current State of Young Adult Literature." *Journal of Youth Services in Libraries* 8 (1995): 151–164.

Chambers, Aidan. "All of a Tremble to See His Danger." *Signal* 51 (September 1986): 193–212.

———. "The Reader in the Book." *Signal* 23 (May 1977). Reprinted in Aidan Chambers, *Booktalk: Occasional Writing on Literature and Children,* 34–58. London: Bodley Head, 1985.

Chatman, Seymour. *Story and Discourse: Narrative Structure in Fiction and Film.* Ithaca, N.Y.: Cornell UP, 1978.

Chisnell, Steven R. "Language and Meaning in the Postmodern Classroom." *English Journal* 82 (1993): 53–58.

Cixous, Hélène. "The Laugh of the Medusa." *Signs* 1 (summer 1976): 875–893.

Clark, Beverly Lyon. *Regendering the School Story: Sassy Sissies and Tattling Tomboys.* New York: Garland, 1996.

Clausen, Christopher. "Home and Away in Children's Fiction." *Children's Literature* 10 (1982): 141–152.

Coats, Karen. "Lacan with Runt Pigs." *Children's Literature* 27 (1999): 105–128.

———. "Performing the Subject of Children's Literature." Ph.D. diss., George Washington University, 1998.

Compton, Mary F., and Juanita Skelton. "A Study of Selected Adolescent Problems as Presented in Contemporary Realistic Fiction for Middle School Students." *Adolescence* 17 (fall 1982): 637–645.

Connell, R. W. *Gender and Power: Society, the Person, and Sexual Politics.* Stanford: Stanford UP, 1987.

Dalsimer, Katherine. *Female Adolescence: Psychoanalytic Reflections on Works of Literature.* New Haven: Yale UP, 1986.

Daly, Mary. *Gyn/Ecology: The Metaethics of Radical Feminism.* 1978. Boston: Beacon, 1990.

DeLuca, Geraldine. "Taking True Risks: Controversial Issues in New Young Adult Novels." *Lion and the Unicorn* 3 (1979): 125–148.

———. "Unself-Conscious Voices: Larger Contexts for Adolescents." *Lion and the Unicorn* 2.2 (1978): 89–108.

DeLuca, Geraldine, and Roni Natov. "An Interview with Robert Cormier." *Lion and the Unicorn* 2.2 (1978): 109–135.

Dixon, Bob. *Political Ideas in Children's Fiction.* Vol. 2 of *Catching Them Young.* London: Pluto, 1977.

———. *Sex, Race, and Class in Children's Fiction.* Vol. 1 of *Catching Them Young.* London: Pluto, 1977.

Dollimore, Jonathan. "The Dominant and the Deviant: A Violent Dialectic." *Critical Quarterly* 28 (1986): 179–192. Reprinted in *Homosexual Themes in Literary Studies,* edited by Wayne R. Dynes and Stephen Donaldson, 87–100. New York: Garland, 1992.

Donelson, Kenneth L., and Alleen Pace Nilsen. *Literature for Today's Young Adults.* 5th ed. New York: Longman, 1997.

Eagleton, Terry. *Criticism and Ideology: A Study in Marxist Literary Theory.* London: Redwood, 1975.

Ecroyd, Catherine Ann. "Growing Up Female." *ALAN Review* 17 (1989): 5–8.

*English Journal.* "Adolescent Literature Comes of Age: From *Little Women* to *Forever.*" 81.4 (April 1992).

Estes, Angela M., and Kathleen M. Lant. "Dismembering the Text: The Horror of Louisa May Alcott's *Little Women.*" *Children's Literature* 17 (1989): 98–123.

Fellman, Anita Clair. "'Don't Expect to Depend on Anybody Else': The Frontier as Portrayed in the Little House Books." *Children's Literature* 24 (1996): 101–116.

Fetterley, Judith. *The Resisting Reader: A Feminist Approach to American Fiction*. Bloomington: Indiana UP, 1978.

Fiedler, Leslie. "Come Back to the Raft Ag'in, Huck Honey!" Reprinted in *The Collected Essays of Leslie Fiedler*, vol. 1, 142–151. New York: Stein and Day, 1971.

Fink, Bruce. *The Lacanian Subject: Between Language and Jouissance*. Princeton: Princeton UP, 1995.

Fish, Stanley. *Is There a Text in This Class?* Cambridge, Mass.: Harvard UP, 1982.

Ford, Elizabeth A. "H/Z: Why Lesléa Newman Makes Heather into Zoe." *Children's Literature Association Quarterly* 23 (1998): 128–133.

Foster, Shirley, and Judy Simons. *What Katy Read: Feminist Re-Readings of "Classic" Stories for Girls*. Iowa City: U of Iowa P, 1995.

Foucault, Michel. *Discipline and Punish: The Birth of the Prison*. Translated by Alan Sheridan. New York: Vintage, 1979.

———. *The History of Sexuality: An Introduction, Volume I*. Translated by Robert Hurley. 1978. New York: Vintage, 1990.

———. *The Order of Things: An Archaeology of the Human Sciences*. 1966. New York: Random House, 1970.

———. *Power/Knowledge: Selected Interviews and Other Writings, 1972–1977*. Edited by Colin Gordon. New York: Pantheon, 1980.

———. "What Is an Author?" In *Language, Counter-Memory, Practice: Selected Essays and Interviews*, edited by Donald F. Bouchard and translated by Bouchard and Sherry Simon, 113–138. Ithaca, N.Y.: Cornell UP, 1977.

French, Marilyn. *Beyond Power: On Women, Men, and Morals*. New York: Summit, 1985.

Frye, Marilyn. "The Necessity of Differences: Constructing a Positive Category of Women." *Signs* 21 (1996): 991-1010.

Fuoss, Kirk. "A Portrait of the Adolescent as a Young Gay: The Politics of Male Homosexuality in Young Adult Fiction." In *Queer Words, Queer Images: Communication and the Construction of Homosexuality*, edited by R. Jeffrey Ringer, 159–174. New York: New York UP, 1994.

Gates, Henry Louis, Jr. *The Signifying Monkey: A Theory of Afro-American Literary Criticism*. New York: Oxford UP, 1988.

Genette, Gérard. *Narrative Discourse: An Essay in Method*. Translated by Jane E. Lewin. Ithaca, N.Y.: Cornell UP, 1980. Translation of "Discours du recit" from *Figures 3* (Paris: Seuil, 1972).

Gilligan, Carol. *In a Different Voice: Psychological Theory and Women's Development*. Cambridge: Harvard UP, 1982.

Giroux, Henry A. "Rethinking the Boundaries of Educational Discourse: Modernism, Postmodernism, and Feminism." *College Literature* 17 (1990): 1–50.

———. "Slacking Off: Border Youth and Postmodern Education." *Journal of Advanced Composition* 14 (1994): 347–366.

Grenz, Dagmar. "Literature for Young People and the Novel of Adolescence." In *Aspects and Issues in the History of Children's Literature*, edited by Maria Nikolajeva, 173–182. Westport, Conn.: Greenwood, 1995.

Hall, G. Stanley. *Adolescence: Its Psychology and Its Relations to Anthropology, Sociology, Sex Crime, Religion, and Education*. 2 vols. New York: Appleton, 1905.

Hatfield, Len. "From Master to Brother: Shifting the Balance of Authority in Ursula K. Le Guin's *Farthest Shore* and *Tehanu*." *Children's Literature* 21 (1993): 43–65.

Heidegger, Martin. *Being and Time*. 1927. Translated by John Macquarrie and Edward Robinson. New York: Harper and Row, 1962.

Henderson, Mae Gwendolyn. "Speaking in Tongues: Dialogics, Dialectics, and the Black Woman Writer's Literary Tradition." In *Changing Our Own Words: Essays on Criticism, Theory, and Writing by Black Women*, edited by Cheryl A. Wall, 16–37. New Brunswick: Rutgers UP, 1989.

Hirsch, Marianne. *Family Frames: Photography, Narrative, and Postmemory*. Cambridge: Harvard UP, 1997.

Hollindale, Peter. "The Adolescent Novel of Ideas." *Children's Literature in Education* 26 (1995): 83–95. Reprinted in *Only Connect: Readings on Children's Literature*, 3d ed., edited by Sheila Egoff, Gordon Stubbs, Ralph Ashley, and Wendy Sutton, 315–326. New York: Oxford UP, 1996.

———. "Ideology and the Children's Book." *Signal* 55 (1988): 3–22.

———. *Signs of Childness in Children's Books*. Stroud, Glos., England: Thimble Press, 1997.

Howe, Susanne. *Wilhelm Meister and His English Kinsmen: Apprentices to Life*. 1930. New York: AMS Press, 1966.

Hunt, Caroline. "Young Adult Literature Evades the Theorists." *Children's Literature Association Quarterly* 21 (1996): 4–11.

Hunt, Peter. *Criticism, Theory, and Children's Literature*. Cambridge: Basil Blackwell, 1991.

Iser, Wolfgang. *Act of Reading: A Theory of Aesthetic Response*. Baltimore: Johns Hopkins UP, 1980.

Jameson, Fredric. *The Political Unconscious: Narrative as a Socially Symbolic Act*. Ithaca, N.Y.: Cornell UP, 1981.

———. *Postmodernism: Or, the Cultural Logic of Late Capitalism*. Durham, N.C.: Duke UP, 1991.

Janeway, Elizabeth. *Man's World, Woman's Place: A Study in Social Mythology*. New York: Morrow, 1971.

Jenkins, Christine. "Heartthrobs & Heartbreaks: A Guide to Young Adult Books with Gay Themes." *Out/Look* (1988): 82–92. Reprinted in *Homosexual Themes in Literary Studies*, edited by Wayne R. Dynes and Stephen Donaldson, 180–191. New York: Garland, 1992.

Johnson, Barbara. *A World of Difference*. Baltimore: Johns Hopkins UP, 1987.

Kett, Joseph F. *Rites of Passage: Adolescence in America, 1790 to the Present*. New York: Basic, 1977.

Keyser, Elizabeth. *Whispers in the Dark: The Fiction of Louisa May Alcott*. Knoxville: U of Tennessee P, 1993.

Kidd, Kenneth. "Introduction: Lesbian/Gay Literature for Children and Young Adults." *Children's Literature Association Quarterly* 23 (1998): 114–119.

Knoeller, Christian P. *Voicing Ourselves: Whose Words We Use When We Talk about Books*. Albany: State U of New York P, 1998.

Kornfeld, Eve, and Susan Jackson. "The Female Bildungsroman in Nineteenth-Century America: Parameters of a Vision." *Journal of American Culture* 10.4 (1987): 69–75.

Kraus, W. Keith. "Still Dreaming and Losing." *School Library Journal* 21 (January 1975): 18–22.

Kristeva, Julia. "Women's Time." *Signs* 7 (1981): 13–35.

Kübler-Ross, Elisabeth. *On Death and Dying*. New York: Macmillan, 1969.

Lacan, Jacques. *Écrits: A Selection*. Translated by Alan Sheridan. New York: Norton, 1977.

———. *The Four Fundamental Concepts of Psycho-Analysis*. Translated by Alan Sheridan and edited by Jacques-Alain Miller. New York: Norton, 1978.

———. "Science and Truth." *Newsletter of the Freudian Field* 3 (1989): 4–29.

Lanser, Susan S. "Toward a Feminist Narratology." *Style* 20.3 (fall 1986): 341–363.

Lawrence-Pietroni, Anna. "*The Tricksters, The Changeover*, and the Fluidity of Adolescent Literature." *Children's Literature Association Quarterly* 21 (1996): 34–39.

Lee, Vanessa Wayne. "'Unshelter Me': The Emerging Fictional Adolescent Lesbian." *Children's Literature Association Quarterly* 23 (1998): 152–159.

Lesnik-Oberstein, Karín. *Children's Literature: Criticism and the Fictional Child*. Oxford: Clarendon, 1994.

Linn, Ray. *A Teacher's Introduction to Postmodernism*. Urbana, Ill.: National Council of Teachers of English, 1996.

Littlefield, Henry M. "The Wizard of Oz: Parable on Populism." *American Quarterly* 16 (1964): 47–58.

Lukens, Rebecca J. "From Salinger to Cormier: Disillusionment to Despair in Thirty Years." *ALAN Review* 9 (1981): 42.

Lukens, Rebecca J., and Ruth K. J. Cline. *A Critical Handbook of Literature for Young Adults*. New York: HarperCollins, 1995.

MacLeod, Anne Scott. "Robert Cormier and the Adolescent Novel." *Children's Literature in Education* 12 (1981): 74–81.

Makaryk, Irena R. *Encyclopedia of Contemporary Literary Theory: Approaches, Scholars, Terms*. Toronto: U of Toronto P, 1993.

Martin, Michelle H. "Periods, Parody, and Polyphony: Fifty Years of Menstrual Education through Fiction and Film." *Children's Literature Association Quarterly* 22 (1997): 21–29.

———. "Periods, Parody, and Polyphony: Ideology and Heteroglossia in Menstrual Education." Ph.D. diss., Illinois State University, 1997.

May, Jill P. *Children's Literature and Critical Theory: Reading and Writing for Understanding.* New York: Oxford UP, 1995.

McGillis, Roderick. "Another Kick at La/can: 'I Am a Picture.'" *Children's Literature Association Quarterly* 20 (1995): 42–46.

———. *The Nimble Reader: Literary Theory and Children's Literature.* New York: Twayne, 1996.

McGowan, John. "Postmodernism." In *Johns Hopkins Guide to Literary Theory and Criticism*, edited by Michael Groden and Martin Kreiswirth, 585–587. Baltimore: Johns Hopkins UP, 1994.

———. *Postmodernism and Its Critics.* Ithaca, N.Y.: Cornell UP, 1991.

McNay, Lois. *Foucault and Feminism: Power, Gender and the Self.* Boston: Northeastern UP, 1992.

Mikkelsen, Nina. "A Conversation with Virginia Hamilton." *Journal of Youth Services in Libraries* 7 (1994): 382–405.

———. *Virginia Hamilton.* New York: Twayne, 1994.

Mo, Wei-Min, and Wenju Shen. "The Twenty-Four Paragons of Filial Piety: Their Didactic Role and Impact on Children's Lives." *Children's Literature Association Quarterly* 24 (1999): 15–23.

Monro, David. *Argument of Laughter.* Carlton, Victoria, Australia: Melbourne UP, 1951.

Moore, Opal, and Donnarae MacCann. "The Uncle Remus Travesty, Part II: Julius Lester and Virginia Hamilton." *Children's Literature Association Quarterly* 11 (1996): 205–210.

Moore, Rebecca Cabell. "Boarding School Books: A Unique Literary Opportunity." *Journal of Youth Services in Libraries* 6 (1993): 378–386.

Murphy, Ann B. "The Borders of Ethical, Erotic, and Artistic Possibilities in *Little Women.*" *Signs* 15 (1990): 562–585.

Myers, Mitzi. "Impeccable Governesses, Rational Dames, and Moral Mothers: Mary Wollstonecraft and the Female Tradition in Georgian Children's Books." *Children's Literature* 14 (1986): 31–59.

———. "Reading Children and Homeopathic Romanticism: Paradigm Lost, Revisionary Gleam, or 'Plus Ça Change, Plus C'est La Même Chose'?" In *Literature and the Child: Romantic Continuations, Postmodern Contestations*, edited by James Holt McGavran, 44–84. Iowa City: U of Iowa P, 1999.

Natov, Roni. "Mothers and Daughters: Jamaica Kincaid's Pre-Oedipal Narrative." *Children's Literature* 18 (1990): 1–16.

Nelms, Ben F. "From *Little Women* to *Forever.*" *English Journal* (April 1992): 9, 11.

Nikolajeva, Maria. *Children's Literature Comes of Age: Toward a New Aesthetic.* New York: Garland, 1996.

Nodelman, Perry. "Balancing Acts: Noteworthy American Fiction." In *Touchstones: Reflections on the Best in Children's Literature*, vol. 3., edited by

Perry Nodelman, 164–171. West Lafayette: Children's Literature Association, 1989.

———. "How Typical Children Read Typical Books." *Children's Literature in Education* 12 (1977): 177–185.

———. *The Pleasures of Children's Literature.* 2d ed. New York: Addison-Wesley, 1995.

———. "Robert Cormier Does a Number." *Children's Literature in Education* 14 (1983): 94–103.

Olson, Marilynn. "In the Throes of Definition." *Children's Literature Association Quarterly* 18 (1993): 2–3.

Orenstein, Peggy. *School Girls: Young Women, Self-Esteem, and the Confidence Gap.* 1994. New York: Anchor, 1995.

Paul, Lissa. "Enigma Variations: What Feminist Theory Knows about Children's Literature." *Signal* 54 (1987): 186–201.

———. *Reading Otherways.* Stroud, Glos., England: Thimble Press, 1998.

Peck, Richard. "The Silver Anniversary of Young Adult Books." *Journal of Youth Services in Libraries* 7 (1993): 19–23.

Pirie, Bruce. *Reshaping High School English.* Urbana, Ill.: National Council of Teachers of English, 1997.

Poe, Elizabeth Ann, Barbara G. Samuels, and Betty Carter. "Twenty-Five Years of Research in Young Adult Literature: Past Perspectives and Future Directions." *Journal of Youth Services in Libraries* 7 (1993): 65–73.

Pratt, Annis. *Archetypal Patterns in Women's Fiction.* Bloomington: Indiana UP, 1981.

Quigly, Isabel. *The Heirs of Tom Brown: The English School Story.* London: Chatto and Windus, 1982.

Ramazanoglu, Caroline. Introduction to *Up against Foucault: Explorations of Some Tensions between Foucault and Feminism.* Edited by Caroline Ramazanoglu, 1–25. New York: Routledge, 1993.

Richards, Jeffrey. "The School Story." In *Stories and Society: Children's Literature in its Social Context,* edited by Dennis Butts, 1–21. London: Macmillan, 1992.

Rose, Jacqueline. *The Case of Peter Pan, or the Impossibility of Children's Fiction.* London: Macmillan, 1984.

Russell, David L. "The Comic Spirit and Cosmic Order in Children's Literature." *Children's Literature Association Quarterly* 15 (1990): 117–119.

Saussure, Ferdinand de. *Course in General Linguistics.* 1915. New York: McGraw-Hill, 1966.

Schwartz, Sheila. *Teaching Adolescent Literature: A Humanistic Approach.* Rochelle Park, N.J.: Hayden, 1979.

Schweickart, Patrocinio P. "Reading Ourselves: Toward a Feminist Theory of Reading." In *Gender and Reading: Essays on Readers, Texts, and Contexts,* edited by Elizabeth A. Flynn and Patrocinio P. Schweickart, 31–62. Baltimore: Johns Hopkins UP, 1986.

Small, Robert C., Jr. "The Literary Value of the Young Adult Novel." *Journal of Youth Services in Libraries* 6 (1992): 277–285.

Sontag, Susan. *On Photography.* New York: Farrar, Straus, Giroux, 1973.

Soper, Kate. "Productive Contradictions." In *Up Against Foucault: Explorations of Some Tensions between Foucault and Feminism,* edited by Caroline Ramazanoglu, 99–122. New York: Routledge, 1993.

Spacks, Patricia Meyer. *The Adolescent Idea: Myths of Youth and the Adult Imagination.* New York: Basic, 1981.

Steig, Michael. "Never Going Home: Reflections on Reading, Adulthood, and the Possibility of Children's Literature." *Children's Literature Association Quarterly* 18 (1993): 36–39.

Stephens, John. *Language and Ideology in Children's Fiction.* New York: Longman, 1992.

Stock, Patricia Lambert. "Post-Modern Scholarship: Contributions from a Practice Profession." *English Education* 28 (1996): 227–251.

Stott, Jon C., and Christine Doyle Francis. "'Home' and 'Not Home' in Children's Stories: Getting There—and Being Worth It." *Children's Literature in Education* 24 (1993): 223–233.

Susina, Jan. "*The Chocolate War* and the Sweet Science." *Children's Literature in Education* 22 (1991): 169–177.

Sutherland, Robert D. "Hidden Persuaders: Political Ideologies in Literature for Children." *Children's Literature in Education* 16 (1985): 143–157.

Tarr, C. Anita. "Does *The Chocolate War* Still Exemplify YA Lit? Did It Ever? Or, I Come to Bury Cormier, Not to Praise Him." Midwest Modern Language Association, Chicago, November 5, 1997.

———. "An Unintentional System of Gaps: A Phenomenological Reading of Scott O'Dell's *Island of the Blue Dolphins.*" *Children's Literature in Education* 28 (1997): 61–71.

Tennyson, G. B. "The *Bildungsroman* in Nineteenth-Century English Literature." In *Medieval Epic to the "Epic Theater" of Brecht,* edited by Rosario P. Armato and John M. Spalek, 135–146. Los Angeles: U of Southern California P, 1968.

Tolson, Nancy D. "Regional Outreach and an Evolving Black Aesthetic." *Children's Literature Association Quarterly* 20 (1995–1996): 183–185.

Travis, Molly Abel. "*Beloved* and *Middle Passage*: Race, Narrative, and the Critic's Essentialism." *Narrative* 2 (1994): 179–200.

Trites, Roberta Seelinger. "'I double never ever never lie to my chil'ren': Inside People in Virginia Hamilton's Narratives." *African American Review* 32 (1998): 147–157.

———. "Theories and Possibilities of Adolescent Literature." *Children's Literature Association Quarterly* 21 (1996): 2–3.

———. *Waking Sleeping Beauty: Feminist Voices in Children's Novels.* Iowa City: U of Iowa P, 1997.

Vallone, Lynne. *Disciplines of Virtue: Girls' Culture in the Eighteenth and Nineteenth Centuries.* New Haven: Yale UP, 1995.

Vandergrift, Kay E. *Mosaics of Meaning: Enhancing the Intellectual Life of Young Adults through Story*. Lanham, Md.: Scarecrow, 1996.

Waddey, Lucy E. "Homes in Children's Fiction: Three Patterns." *Children's Literature Association Quarterly* 8 (1983): 13–15.

Weber, Max. *Max Weber on Law in Economy and Society*. Edited by Max Rheinstein and translated by Edward Shils. Cambridge: Harvard UP, 1966.

Weeks, Jeffrey. *Sexuality and Its Discontents: Meanings, Myths and Modern Sexualities*. London: Routledge and Kegan Paul, 1985.

West, Cornel. *Keeping Faith: Philosophy and Race in America*. New York: Routledge, 1993.

West, Mark I. "The Grotesque and the Taboo in Roald Dahl's Humorous Writings for Children." *Children's Literature Association Quarterly* 15 (1990): 115–116.

White, Barbara A. *Growing Up Female: Adolescent Girlhood in American Fiction*. Westport, Conn.: Greenwood, 1985.

Wiegman, Robyn. *American Anatomies: Theorizing Race and Gender*. Durham, N.C.: Duke UP, 1995.

Wilson, Sharon R. "Camera Images in Margaret Atwood's Novels." In *Margaret Atwood: Reflection and Reality*, edited by Beatrice Mendez-Egle and James M. Haule, 29–57. Edinburg, Tex.: Pan American University, 1987.

Winnett, Susan. "Coming Unstrung: Women, Men, Narrative, and Principles of Pleasure." *PMLA* 105 (1990): 505–518.

Wood, Naomi. "Introduction: Children's Literature and Religion." *Children's Literature Association Quarterly* 24 (1999): 1–3.

Yoshida, Junko. "The Quest for Masculinity in *The Chocolate War*: Changing Conceptions of Masculinity in the 1970s." *Children's Literature* 26 (1998): 105–122.

# Index